ROB KRIER

ON ARCHITECTURE

ROB KRIER

ON ARCHITECTURE

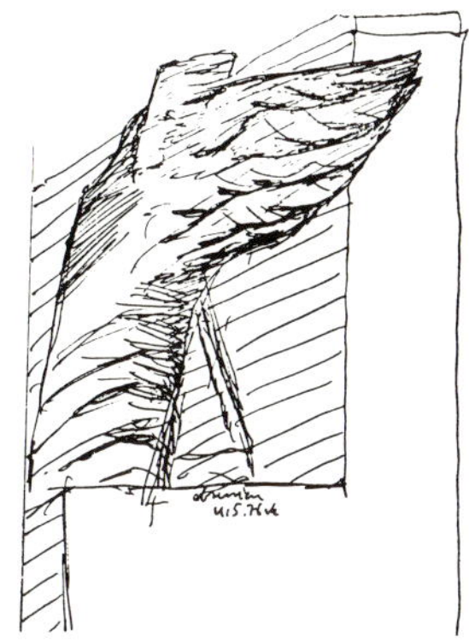

CONTENTS

ACADEMY EDITIONS · LONDON

ST. MARTIN'S PRESS · NEW YORK

L'ordre est le plaisir de la raison
Le désordre est le délice de l'imagination
Paul Valéry

Back cover
Redesign of the 'Via Triumphalis', Karlsruhe 1979, aerial perspective

Frontispiece
Sketches for interiors

First published in Great Britain in 1982 by
Academy Editions 7/8 Holland Street London W8

Published in the United States of America in 1982 by
St. Martin's Press 175 Fifth Avenue New York NY 10010

Library of Congress Catalog Card Number 82-60004
ISBN 0-312-68541-6 Cloth ISBN 0-312-68542-4 Paper

Translated from the German by Eileen Martin

Phototypeset by Tradespools Ltd., Frome, Somerset
Printed and bound in Hong Kong

Rob Krier
10 THESES ON ARCHITECTURE

These principles have applied since man began to plan his buildings rationally and see architecture as an aesthetic product, that is, give his building form beyond its useful purpose.

1
FUNCTION, CONSTRUCTION AND FORM
are of equal value and together determine the architecture. None should have priority over the others.

2
FUNCTION AND CONSTRUCTION
are elements of a useful nature whose fulfilment should be a matter of course in building. Only when they are raised to an aesthetic level does a building become architecture.

3
THE MEANS OF AESTHETIC SUBLIMATION ARE:
— Proportion
— Structure
— The handling of materials and colour and the artistic interpretation of these.

4
THE AESTHETIC DIMENSION
The deeper significance of beauty in architecture lies in man's need to give his useful objects a poetic dimension which will communicate the 'spirit' of his age to future generations.
("... it is useful because it is beautiful ..." Antoine de Saint-Exupéry)

5
GEOMETRY
is the basis of all architectural articulation. As organised geometry, architecture derives its force from the contrast with living nature, not from a formal adjustment to it. Architecture is the creation of man.

6
SCALE
in architecture should be adjusted to the size of the human body and its patterns of behaviour, perception and sensitivity. It should not be orientated to technical or structural principles or to economic considerations only.

7
URBAN ARCHITECTURE
Any new planning in a city should be such that it fits into the general order and offers a formal response to existing spatial patterns.

8
THE CITY AS A WHOLE
has been forgotten in 20th-century urban planning. Our new cities consist of collections of individual buildings. Five thousand years of urban history show that the complex structures of streets and squares are necessary as communication zones and centres of identity. The modern city needs the traditional concepts of urban planning as well.

9
HISTORY
The proper appreciation of our historical heritage will filter the experience of the past to the advantage of planning for the future.

10
THE RESPONSIBILITY OF THE ARCHITECT
The architect alone is responsible for the product which emerges from his drawing board and bears his signature. No politician or financier will take the cultural blame from the architect's shoulders for a mis-planned environment. It is the responsibility of our universities to prepare future generations of architects for this overwhelming ethical and moral task.

Friedrich Achleitner
ON ROB KRIER

What depresses the unbeliever so much about religious wars is the apparent inability of man to learn from indirect experience, that is, from history. The religious wars in architecture too throw up with monotonous regularity the old prejudices and aggressions against the camp which happens to be holding the dominant journalistic position. In the rather superficial beat of the latest waves, the flood of Catholic sensuality and ebb of Protestant self-denial follow one upon the other: a moralising animosity to form (in positivist and Marxist traditions of thought as well) following with great regularity upon the notoriously 'culinary', often unreflecting world of vision. Reform and counter-reform in architecture follow each other like night and day, and as it all happens in different places, at different times and to different rhythms, the predominant condition is that of twilight.

Gottfried Semper could still divide architects into three groups—materialists, historicists and schematists or purists. Today, the materialists may be historical as well as speculative, the historicists both mathematical and schematic, while the schematists or purists are no less prone to historicism. What they all share is a dream-like over-estimation of the role of architecture, both with regard to its real 'achievement' and the possibilities it has of influencing life. Schools do battle in buildings put up by other schools, and each time they fight as if the world were at stake. Of course the destruction caused to European cities by the Second World War and the opportunity this offered for planning mistakes on a scale never seen before have distorted the perspective a little. Berlin today still offers architects the concrete illusion that urban planning is possible. Nevertheless, we should bear in mind the purely quantitative relation between the existing stock of buildings and the volume which any one generation can add, and above all we should accept the fact that every generation has to live in the buildings its predecessors have left. So far each generation has had to come to terms with this historical inheritance, this 'inherent determinism'; they have all set up house and lived their different social lives here. One of the most fatal illusions of functionalism was the belief that there is unity between architectural form and social life, indeed the delusion that architecture can give elementary expression to life and is capable of forming it.

As early as 1930 Josef Frank in Vienna argued that a house which was easy and pleasant to live in could be built in any style. We could put it differently today: form is not necessarily dependent on purpose, rather its relation to purpose is something which is planned, calculated, voluntary. That is what constitutes its message, and there is always an historical aspect to this. The relation between form and purpose is therefore always an historical relation, and it constitutes only a brief episode in the life of a building. From the moment of its realisation, the reception and interpretation of form will go their own ways while the material existence of the building will offer scope for utilisation and function according to the way it is built, and this can never be fully exhausted by the form. On the other hand, the scope for use can never keep pace with the intellectual dimension of the form, the different roles this will play in the course of history. If this were not so, architectural design would have no historical significance at all. But that also means that in this field architects are concerning themselves with the most transient aspects of the building, a visual phenomenon which will be an historical document the moment the building is finished. Perhaps it is this 'lack of reality' which makes architects so inclined vastly to overestimate their profession. The trivialisation of functionalism would never have been so readily accepted if form really played a primary role in building. The paradox is complete when one recognises that beyond the physical nature of the building only the form can give it permanence, permanence in the sense of an idea once spoken, formulated, whose materialisation (according to Oswald Wiener) is its first repetition.

Since the architectural concept has only a diminishing chance of surviving against the reality of the building, we would appear to have reached that point where the 'architect as designer' (I almost spoke of the 'architect as thinker') changes from being a producer to a consumer, taking on the task of the articulation of unsatisfied desires. And while the heads of architectural factories stamp around exhibitions criticising everything in sight and changing appointments to juries and the editorial boards of architectural periodicals, their minions at the drawing boards are already working on a new vocabulary. So the copyists reach the building stage faster than those whose works are being copied, while the division of labour and the concentration of profit remain unaffected.

It could well be argued that Vienna is not a good place to do justice to the work of Rob Krier. Despite her Baroque and the Ringstrasse, Vienna has little of the basic grammar of urban planning; her historical sensibility (or irritability?) lies more in the sphere of idiom, in the relativity of the half-tones and shades of colour. The poetry of the place, whatever that may be, has emerged with all the variety of a big city from an agglomeration of small villages and it does not show major typological lines of development but rather layering, mixtures, transmutations. The historical element in the city is too omnipresent to be felt as historical.

Whatever Rob Krier's role may have been in the anti- or post-functionalist movement of the 1970s, his work, especially that in Vienna, does raise certain 'existential' questions. If we ignore for the moment the general denunciation of these trends as 'restorative', 'bourgeois-deterministic', there are some criticisms which we simply cannot overlook. The most important of these is that this is an unreflecting use of historical patterns in urban planning, their phenomenological use, so to speak, as a self-contained aesthetic system; historicism without an historical consciousness. It is an accusation that history is present in form but absent in content, indeed that structural planning and political and economic, even technical processes, are excluded. But precisely these have been the main concern of functionalist urban planning (i.e. planning motivated by technology and science) in the last half century. There is also the accusation that this is a positivist, ultimately a Romantic attitude to the profession, affirming as it does the neutrality of historical models and methods of building and pretending that these can be re-created or copied by anyone at any time.

There is more of this confused argument and I can indicate further points of attack: such as the objection that the glorification of the crafts of building betrays a woeful ignorance of the realities of building economics; the belief in a binding grammar and syntax of architecture (which can be learned from text-books); the provocative insistence on the postulated timelessness of certain (but not all) historical phenomena which leads to a schematisation of architectural ideas and ultimately the construction of parameters in relation to an equally unchanging image of man and society.

Although Aldo Rossi in his typological draughtsmanship poetically transforms history while at the same time distancing its collective content as history from the present, this question does not appear to arise for Rob Krier at all. And (this is the worst criticism) while the architect who thinks historically is always at pains to remain at the head of historical development and define his own path through history—in other words to document his distance from it—Rob Krier works outside history insofar as he uses its products as material, as the aesthetic deposits of unreflecting processes, as a treasure-chest of unprocessed experience.

Before attempting to answer this criticism I would like to introduce another aspect into the discussion. One could maintain that Krier's architecture derives from a reality in design rather than from historical tradition. His drawings derive their statement (message, mood) from an undefined, indeed veiled distance to historical scenarios. The moment of concealment, covering up, of what has not been brought to the surface generally plays a major part, especially in the figures. Even the naked figures wear masks, they are masks, behind which more masks appear. And the 'architectural world' which he draws has the character of a scene, a reminiscence produced from movable scenery, often corresponding more to an inner than to an outer reality. We could also speak of a dream world made real, using alienated historical elements and penetrating 'our reality' sometimes more and sometimes less. It is in this sphere that we find the filter to real history, to the living tradition, and to historical truth.

One could argue that this artistic world arises from the opposition to existing buildings, certainly to the aesthetic and intellectual bankruptcy of contemporary architecture and urban planning. It is a hypothetical counter-world whose only chance of being realised is in drawing. This might also explain the unconcealed pathos, the emotion of the presentation, the often depressively monumental mood, a dimension of architectural emotionality which has not been seen before in this form in the field of architecture. But be they psychogram or a counter-world (or the two in one), it is this which gives these drawings the fascination they exercise, their suggestive force.

This is the key which shows the absurdity of the criticism that this is historicising. Krier would appear to concern himself with history only insofar as it guarantees him a certain constancy of spatial experience, and it is with the patterns he derives from this that he calls into question the basis of the current architectural approach. He does not appear to have any intention of learning from history in another sense or of reproducing a specific historical world. His link with history lacks concrete ties to historical processes or truths; the phenomenological basis is sufficient for the renewal and articulation of spatial experience.

The use of classical categories in the formulation of urban spaces, the adaptation of well-proven patterns (streets, squares, courtyards) and their variations, the withdrawal into a 'sane' reliance on the crafts of building, can only be explained through the dialectic between the psychical situation of protest and the architectural reality which has induced it. The proof of this thesis seems to me to lie in Krier's few buildings, and especially the Ritterstrasse housing in Berlin, the architecture of which is a synthesis (not necessarily a compromise) of wishful thinking and what one might describe as contingency. In the building's realisation, the monumentalism of the drawing and the model are lost. The axial structure and the arched entrance create a straightforward, unobtrusive and coherent urban situation. The entrance lobby is on a grand scale and has something of the attraction of urban (bourgeois) entrance halls and stairwells. The typology of the individual apartments is not only 'practicable', that is, utilisable in a number of ways, but it also exercises a spatial fascination—it is architecture in the best and most natural sense of the word. No-one could say that the housing in Ritterstrasse is an historicist building—rather it reflects history, or better, introduces historical spatial experience as a new concept.

This in itself should be sufficient to counter the suspicions and accusations outlined above. If one also considers the over-strained autonomy of architecture, the inherent laws of the medium, then Krier's method of aesthetic reception and reflection appears even more legitimate. If it is not admissible to generalise any architectural or formal principle (or indeed any system in any field whatsoever), or to claim totality for these, then of course the language evolved by Rob Krier is only meaningful within the context of the contemporary scene, from the experience in Stuttgart of an urban landscape planned to death to the problems in Berlin of urban repair, including the criticism of functionalism in the 1970s and the breakaway to an architecture unblinkered by a doctrinaire approach. Today it is all too easy to forget the architectural situation of the 1960s, the unfulfilled hopes of a politicised, technical or scientific architecture and the realities of the economic situation. By its very nature architecture is capable of creating 'complete systems', formalised philosophies, all of which bear the seeds of a claim to totality. Fashions are sometimes subject to such claims with the result that their counter movements ignore their substance. The work of Rob Krier may well produce such an effect (if it has not already been doing so), and it would be a shame if it were to become the victim of such an abstruse dynamic.

In a brief foreword it is not possible to analyse the work of Rob Krier in a wider context. For that we should have not only to consider the continuous dialogue with his brother Leo but also outline his general development over the last ten years. What we have here is more of a snapshot of the discussion which is now taking place in Vienna, and in which Rob Krier is playing a central role as a constant 'point of friction', affectionately jostled, sometimes courted but generally kept from building.

Rob Krier
ON MY PROFESSION

The daily working life of an architect who concerns himself with the practical implementation of his ideas has sunk to a level which holds none of those dreams that once made our profession a major vehicle of culture.

There is hardly a contractor now who is really interested in architecture!

Return on investment is the only motor which drives the building industry. The architecture which our rich and well-fed society produces is shameful beyond words, a reflection of the unmistakable decline in our level of education and culture.

The world is saturated as never before with schools, universities and training centres of every kind; our knowledge about the things of this world should, it would seem, have grown to gigantic levels, but our knowledge of its beauty would appear to have paled in proportion.

Nor will beauty ever be able to grow new roots in a society which is geared to fast consumption, and in which silence, the stuff on which it feeds, is being choked in the intoxication of superficiality.

Beauty is the only thing which inspires me in my profession. I am striving to escape the aridity of simply fulfilling needs and avoid the bitter aftertaste of a desire for profit without any ethical or physical background. Any effort in this direction seems to me a waste of energy.

The veil of ugliness which so tightly encircles our world will take our children's breath away. In view of the terrible catastrophes which our century has brought upon itself, in full awareness of what it was doing, and the even more unfathomable catastrophes it is now in the process of creating, my call for a boycott may well sound like a choked sob.

Why squeeze out the tears?

Everything is going swimmingly! The acres of ruins left by the last wars have been cleared away, and enough old buildings are left to satisfy our nostalgia. In any case, the world looks different from behind our well-tended rose garden. Even I, to my surprise, have quite a few commissions to keep me busy.

In comparison with this optimism I take a rather grim view of the situation.

What has this modern architecture given us?

Which of the buildings of the last few decades have really been of sufficient quality to penetrate the general consciousness? And which can we look at more than once without being bored?

Or to put it differently: if you were showing a visitor around your home town, to which new buildings would you take him?

In every city in the world the percentage of worthy buildings is so low that there is little chance that the layman will know them.

The caprices of modern architecture have become an incestuous problem for specialists. Architecture has lost her cultural role, and with the best will in the world I cannot believe that while modern contractors, in other words politicians, financiers and promoters, are pouring out their private bad taste on land and city, supported by a ruined building craft, a healthy architecture, one we will be proud to pass on as our heritage, can develop. The gags and trick-like alienations which have filled the architectural periodicals in recent years are not likely to point to a solution. On the contrary!

Enforced cheerfulness, a false and unnatural regurgitation of quotations from architectural history are but a withered fig-leaf which cannot conceal our impotence.

The 1960s revealed the need for a more coherent theoretical approach in the social sector. It is now time for architecture to consolidate the theoretical foundation of its own long-established craft, the art of building, to re-discover the basic elements of architecture and the art of composing with them.

We do not need new inventions for this. In the course of history it has all been played out over and over again in countless variations across the continents.

We must always be aware that whatever we do in architecture must be such that it can be handed on. Only then can the chain of experience, of learning from our heritage, be further developed and improved. With this solid, rational basis, genial side-steps can be easily absorbed. Side-steps for their own sake and in overwhelming number, as they have been spat out by our age, can only be a short-lived fashion. The dance of absurdities goes on in full swing, celebrated on all sides as a release.

Our carnival mood will be followed by disillusionment when the bluff has been called and the intoxication is over.

For those who don't want a hangover or can see no way out of the confusion there is an honourable avenue of retreat: as in former times the peasant planned the use of his land carefully and wisely, using certain and unmystifying means and then did the work with his own hands, so should we today, after clarifying the basic issues of architecture, be able to produce an honourable and simple architecture of which no-one need feel ashamed. A precondition is that we should recognise what purpose a door is to serve, a window, a wall, the supports, the roof and so on.

Any layman should be able to recognise these as basic elements. Alienation for the sake of originality is misplaced. In this, modern architecture has taught us a bitter lesson.

The struggle for the basic truth of things, to whose articulation our profession is dedicated, and the longing for beauty, which can enclose our life in the walls we have constructed—these strengthen me and help me to bear the burden of the despair to which I have given utterance here.

FEATURED PROJECTS

Kolbeinsson House
Luxembourg 1975

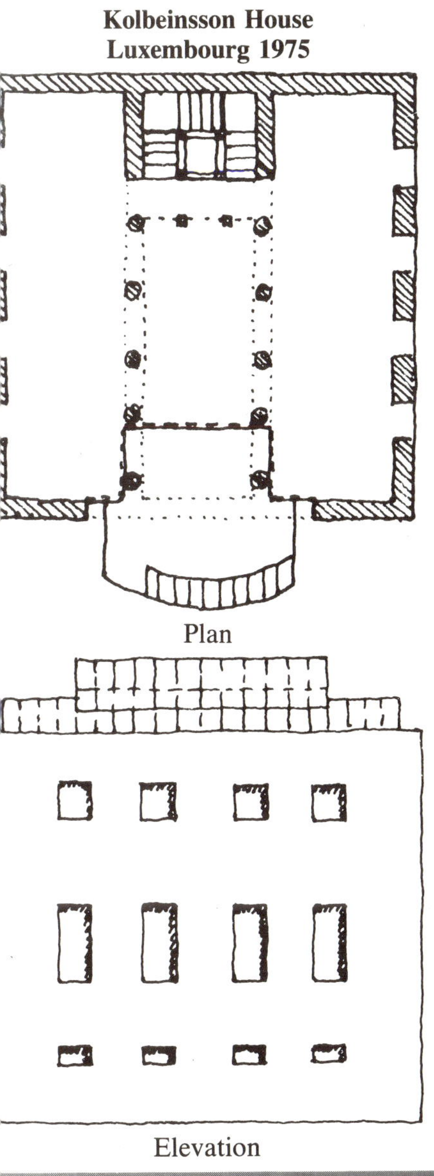

Plan

Elevation

Model

Weidemann House
Stuttgart 1975

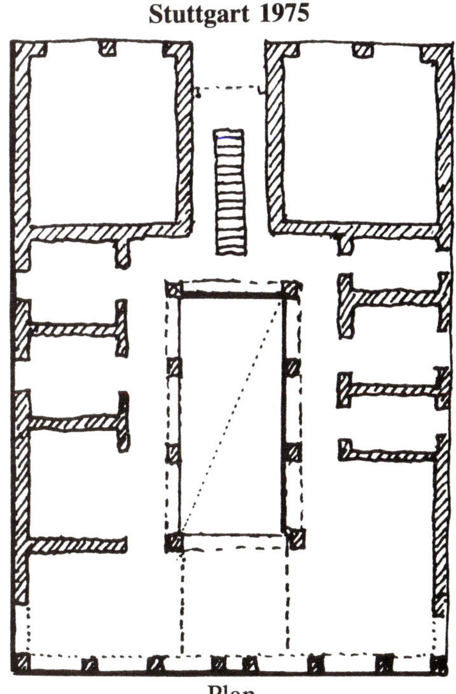

Plan

Model

Model

Community Centre
Brunn am Gebirge 1977

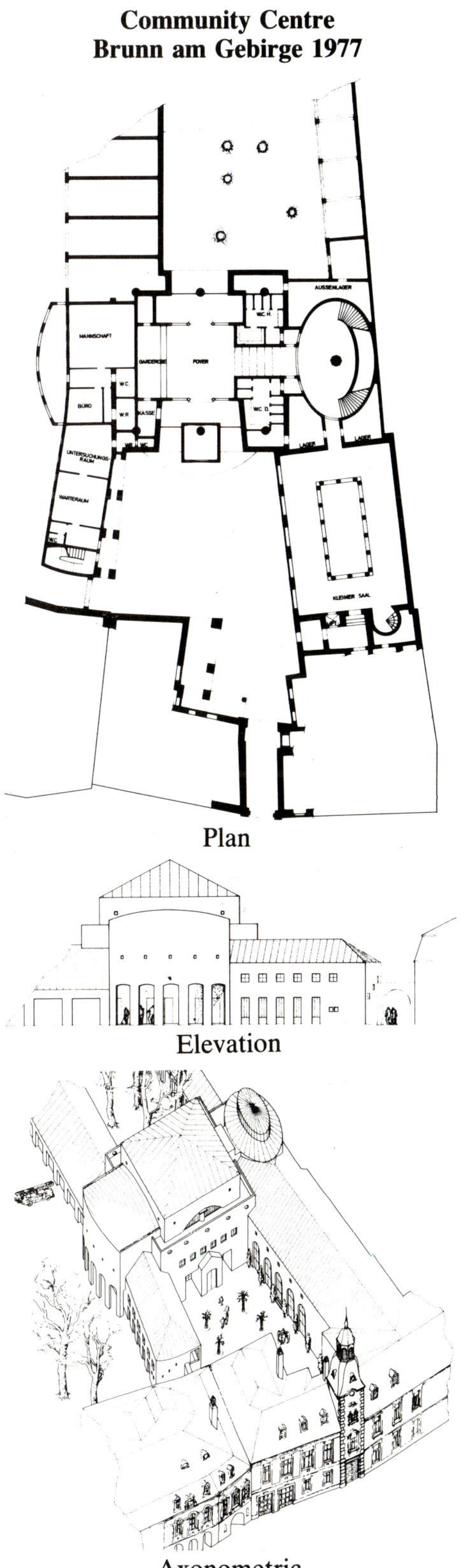

Plan

Elevation

Axonometric

High School
Perchtoldsdorf 1977

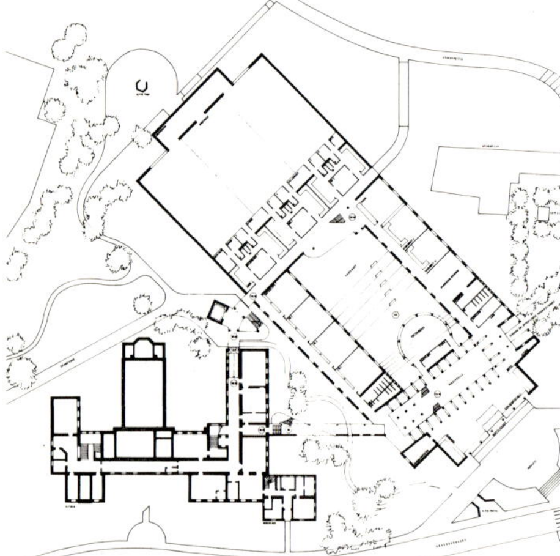
Plan

Model

Hamburg Altona-Nord 1978

Site plan

Residential Area 'Rennweg'
Vienna 1977

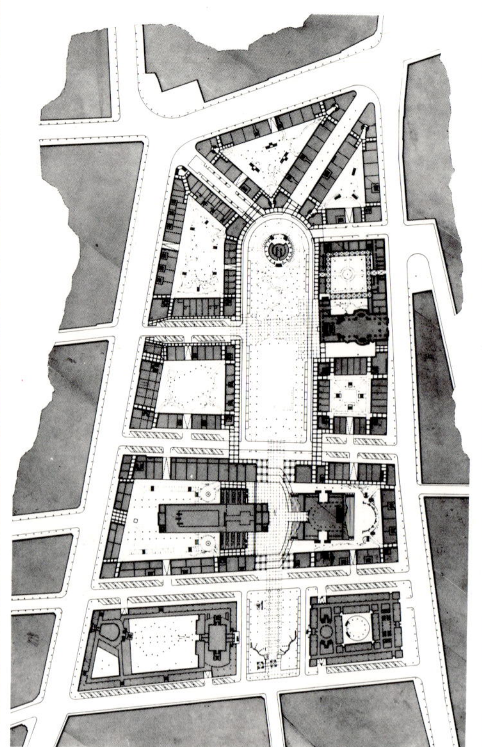
Plan

Model

Lindenstrasse–Alte Jakobstrasse
Berlin 1977–80

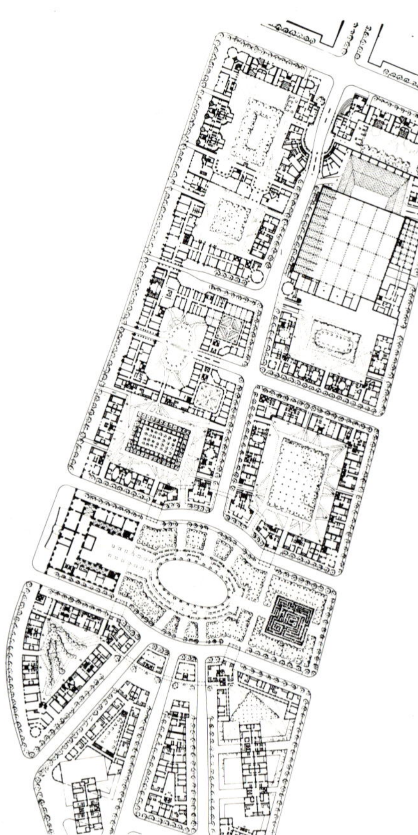
Plan

Model

Schinkelplatz
Berlin 1977–81

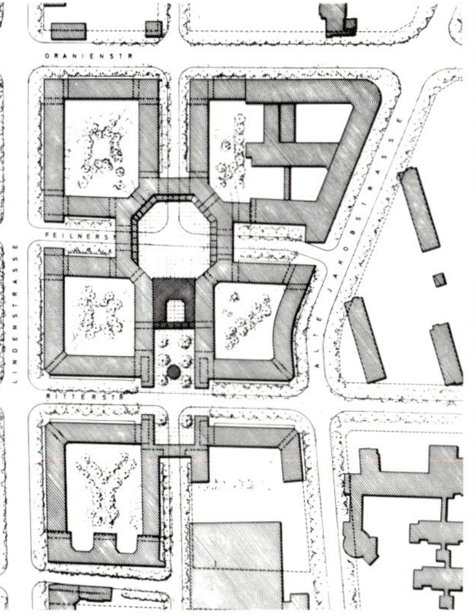

Plan (variation 15)

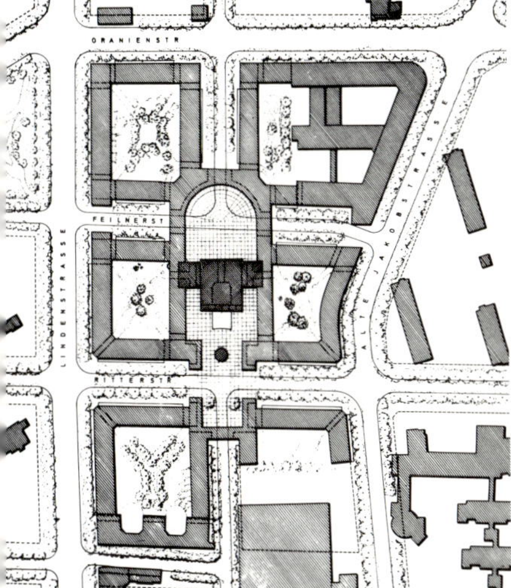

Plan (variation 7)

Model

Ritterstrasse Housing
Berlin 1977–80

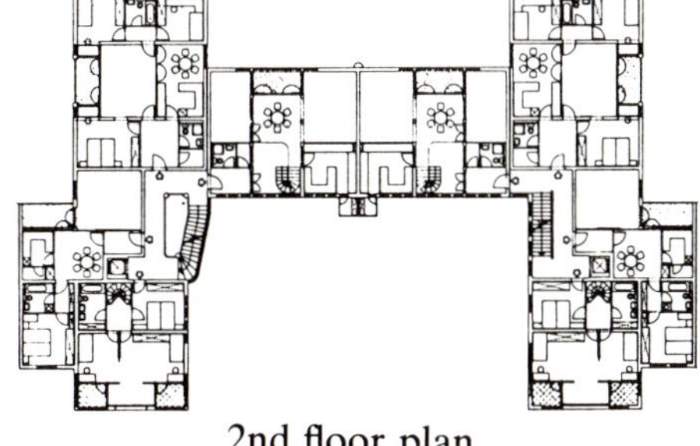

2nd floor plan

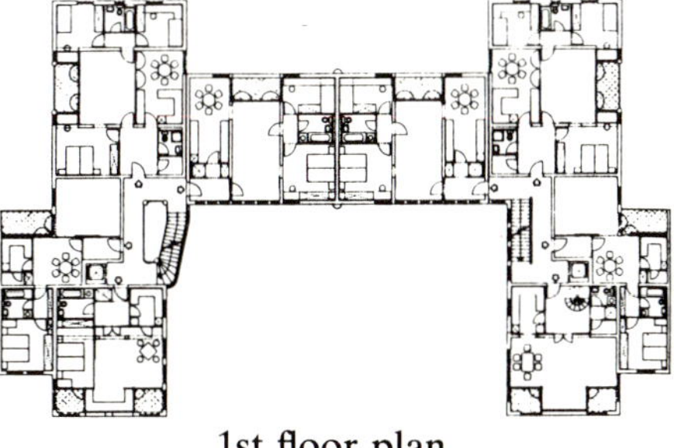

1st floor plan

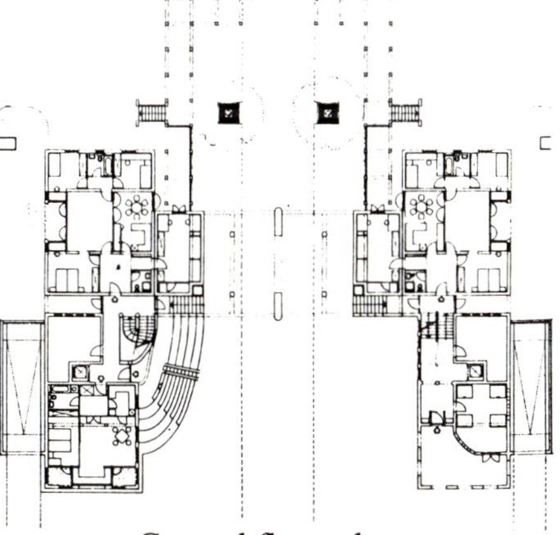

Ground floor plan

Model (front view)

Model (rear view)

Ephraim Palais
Berlin 1979

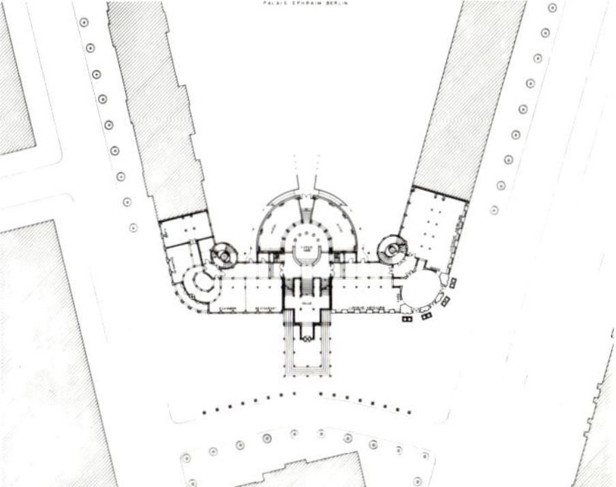

Plan

Facade of the old Palais

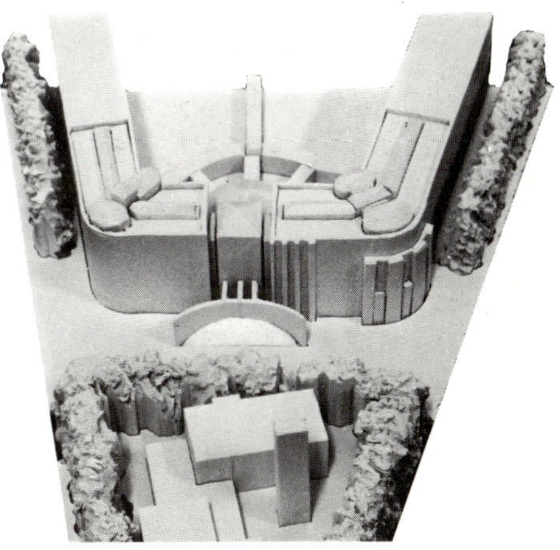

Model

Breitscheidplatz
Berlin 1978

Plan of the area

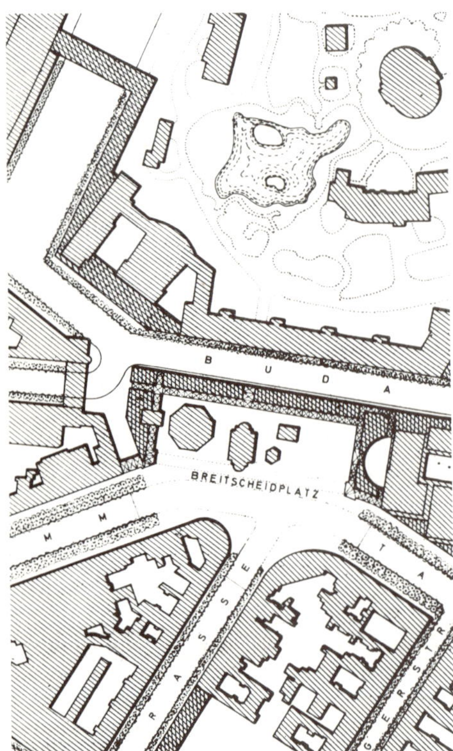

Plan

Model

Prager Platz
Berlin 1978

Street network and block structure

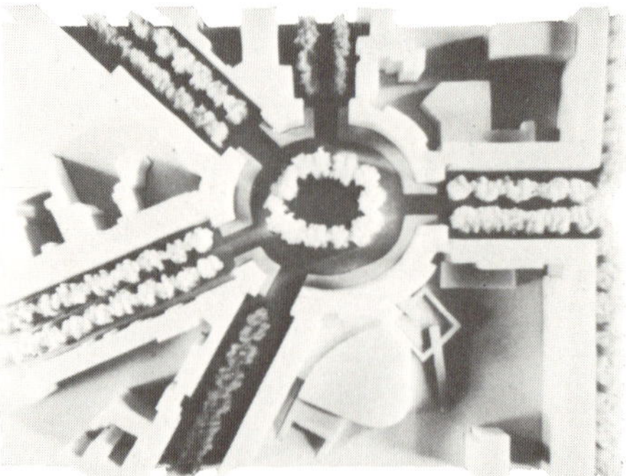

Model (variation 2)

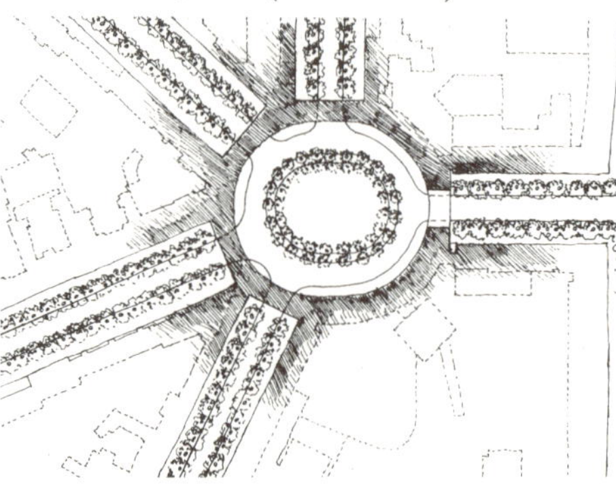

Plan (variation 2)

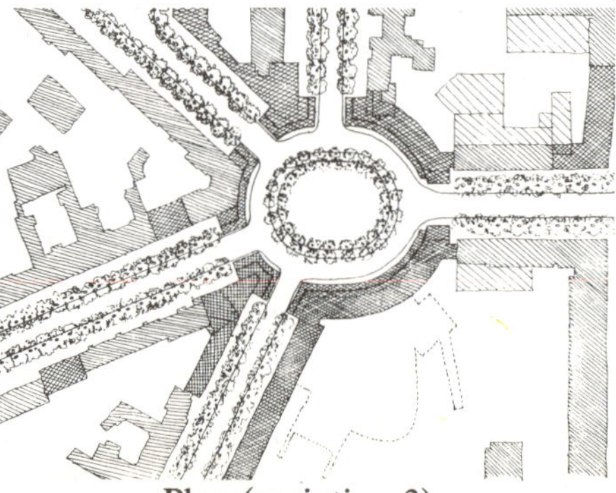

Plan (variation 3)

Lindenufer 34
Berlin Spandau 1978

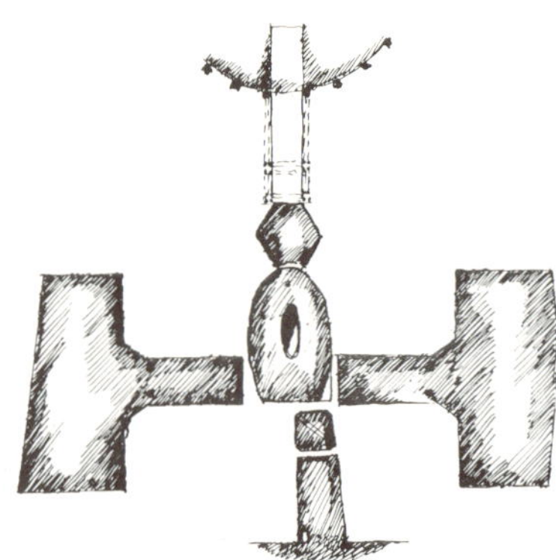

Spatial composition

Model

Model

Lindenufer 31
Berlin Spandau 1979

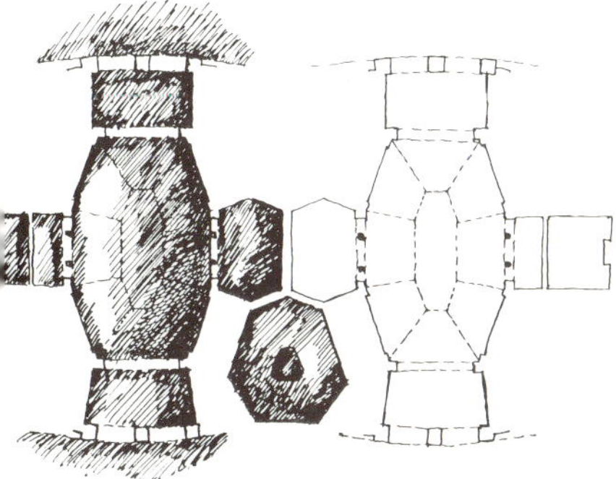

Spatial composition

Model

Model

'Via Triumphalis'
Karlsruhe 1979

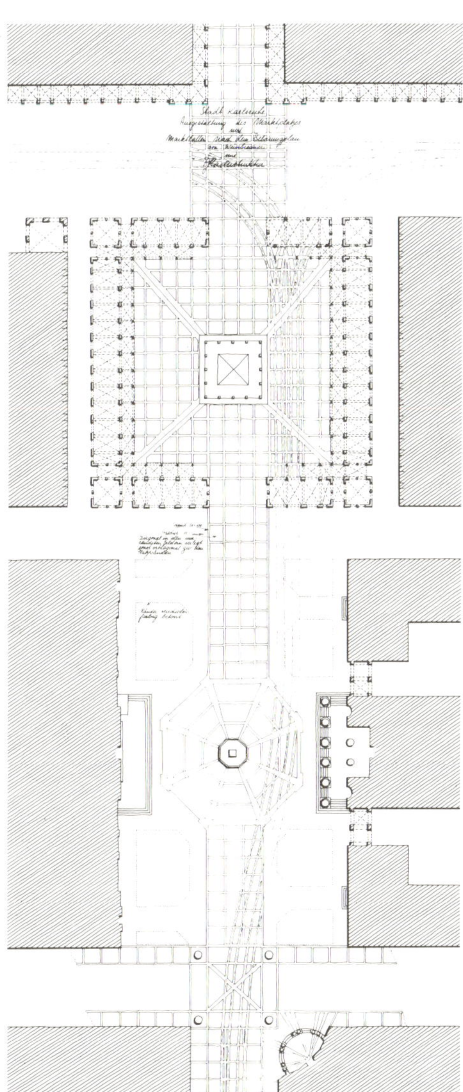

Plan

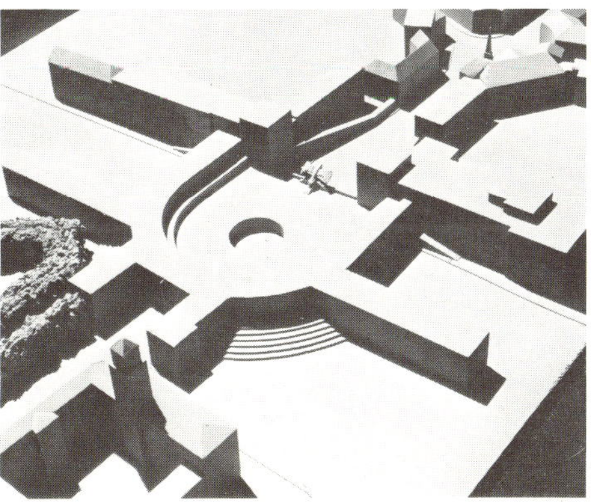

Model of Ettlinger Torplatz

Library
Karlsruhe 1979

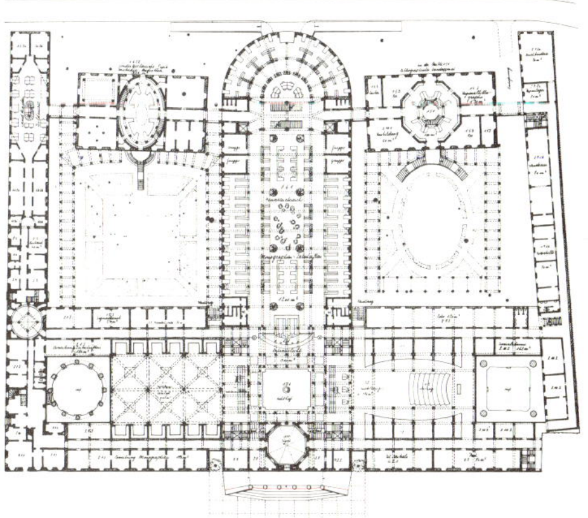

Ground floor plan

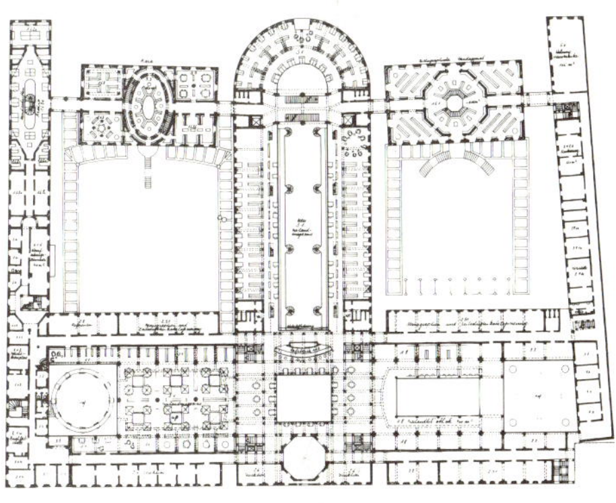

1st floor plan

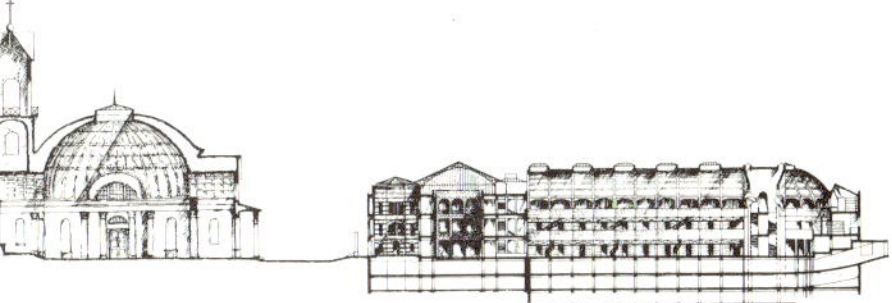

Section through the central axis

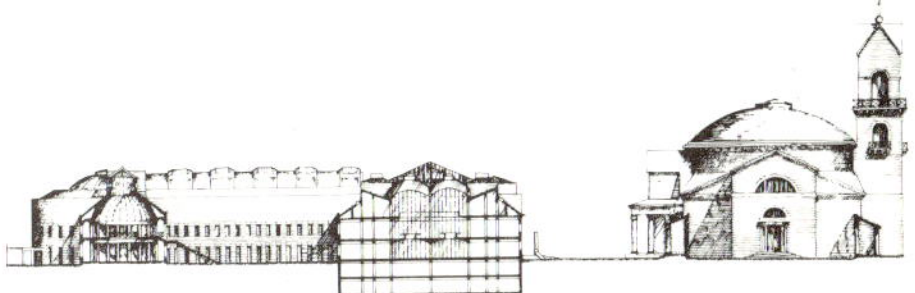

Section through the east courtyard

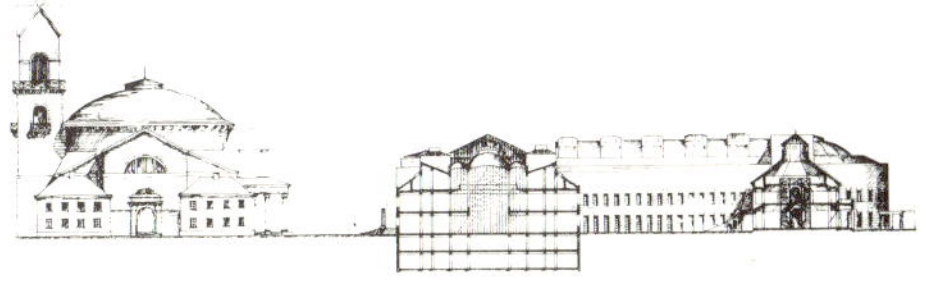

Section through the west courtyard

BIBLIOGRAPHY, EXHIBITIONS AND BUILT WORKS

BIBLIOGRAPHY

Books

Urban Space, Academy Editions, London, 1979, 1980; originally published under the title *Stadtraum in Theorie und Praxis*, Karl Krämer Verlag, Stuttgart, 1975; Gustavo Gili, Barcelona, 1976; A & U, Tokyo, 1980; Archives d'Architecture Moderne, Brussels, 1981

Notizen am Rande, Abakon Verlag, Berlin, 1975

Architectural Composition, Academy Editions, London, (in preparation)

Articles in Periodicals

L'Architecture d'Aujourd'hui:
170 Maison Siemer, 1973
190 Formalisme-Réalisme
198 L'Espace Public
200 Berlin Ritterstrasse
207 Urban Space
213 Berlin Ritterstrasse

Casabella:
378 The Permanence of Form, 1973
382 An Unedited Colossus, 1973
Triennale 73, 1974

Deutsche Bauzeitung:
6 Haus Siemer, Warmbronn, 1973
8 Junge Stuttgarter Architekten

Architectural Review: House Siemer, 1973

Architectural Forum: Haus Siemer, 1973

Nueva Forma: Works of Sculpture and Architecture, 1973

Kajima, Inst. Publ. 6682: House Siemer, 1973

Bouw 49: Haus Siemer, 1973

Ottagono 31: Contribution to the Triennale 73, Milan

Neuf: Architecture des loisirs, 1973

MD Möbeldesign: Rekonstruktion zerstörter Stadträume, 1973

Global Interior: House in Northern Europe, 1974

Bauen und Wohnen: Haus Siemer, 1974; Haus Dickes, 1975

A & U 77/06: Focus Rob Krier

Bauwelt 14/1980: Bibliothek Karlsruhe; Haus Dickes, 1975

Lotus International:
9 Haus Siemer, 1975
11 Krier Brothers, 1976
13 Drawings, 1976
19 Competition Ballhausplatz, 1978
21 Three Exercises, 1978
22 Haus Dickes, 1979
28 Projects for Berlin, 1977–80, 1981

Architectural Design:
49/1 Leon & Rob Krier, 1979
49/3–4 Roma Interrotta, 1979

Werk Bauen + Wohnen June 1980: Berlinprojekte

Neue Heimat 10/8: Berlinprojekte

EXHIBITIONS

1968 University of Stuttgart
1973 Triennale, Milan
1975 Kunstverein, Stuttgart
1976 Technical University, Vienna
1977 Galleria d'Arte Moderna, Bologna
Institute for Architecture and Urban Studies, New York
Architectural Book Store, Los Angeles
Kunstverein, Freiburg
1978 Municipal Planning Office, Karlsruhe
Deutscher Werkbund, Darmstadt
1979 Schools of Architecture in Strasbourg, Nancy and Brussels
1980 Galerie Jannone, Milan
Berlin: Works in the exhibition 'Architectural Drawings from the Renaissance to the Present'
Exhibitions at American universities—New York: Institute for Architecture and Urban Studies; Chicago: Graham Foundation; Detroit: Lawrence Institute of Technology; Minneapolis: University of Minnesota; Seattle: University of Washington; Berkeley: University of California; Houston: University of Texas; Washington D.C.: Smithsonian Institute
Vienna and Innsbruck

BUILT WORKS

House Siemer, Stuttgart, 1968–70
House Dickes, Luxembourg, 1974–75
Social housing in Berlin-Kreuzberg, 1977–80; in Berlin-Spandau (in the course of planning and construction); in Berlin-Wilmersdorf (in the course of planning); Berlin, Schinkelplatz (in the course of planning); Berlin-Tiergarten; and Vienna Liesing (also in the course of planning)

THE ELEMENTS OF ARCHITECTURE

AND SELECTED PROJECTS

Nature Transformed

Carved into the landscape, raised from its coincidental mass, made to serve a useful purpose and

to protect, formed to lend meaning to existence, often maltreated, broken, destroyed beyond hope of regeneration... Time will give a spiritual quality to all stone.

The Wall

The most obvious, perhaps even the most archaic, building technique is to lay stone on stone and

thus to form an homogeneous constructed mass. A long wall must either be thick enough to stand alone or it needs to be supported by a system of pillars, ribs and terracing, outer covering or network.

The Column

This element comes closest to building in wood. In a miraculous filigree Nature has left us a magnificent encyclopedia of possibilities which could be exploited in building. For thousands of years the basic forms of architecture have been given significant interpretation in stone. The

modelling of the shaft, the base and the capital with their complex visual and structural requirements has matured to perfection over the course of time. Modern technology has let these themes perish and reduced them to a primitive vocabulary.

The Bridge

A connecting link across a valley or bearer of supply lines ... this technique has brought magnificent structural achievements. But with a few exceptions, such as Palladio's design for the Rialto Bridge in Venice, the theme has never been treated by classical architecture with the same

devotion as other monumental buildings. The field offers inexhaustible possibilities for powerful gesture. It is a pity that the architects have left it almost entirely to the engineers.

The Roof

A roof suspended on pillars is the simplest kind of protection against the weather, and for centuries has served as barn, store-house, market . . . In Antiquity, the protective roof with the 'cella' beneath became the symbol of the ideal house and the prototype of the temple. This is an

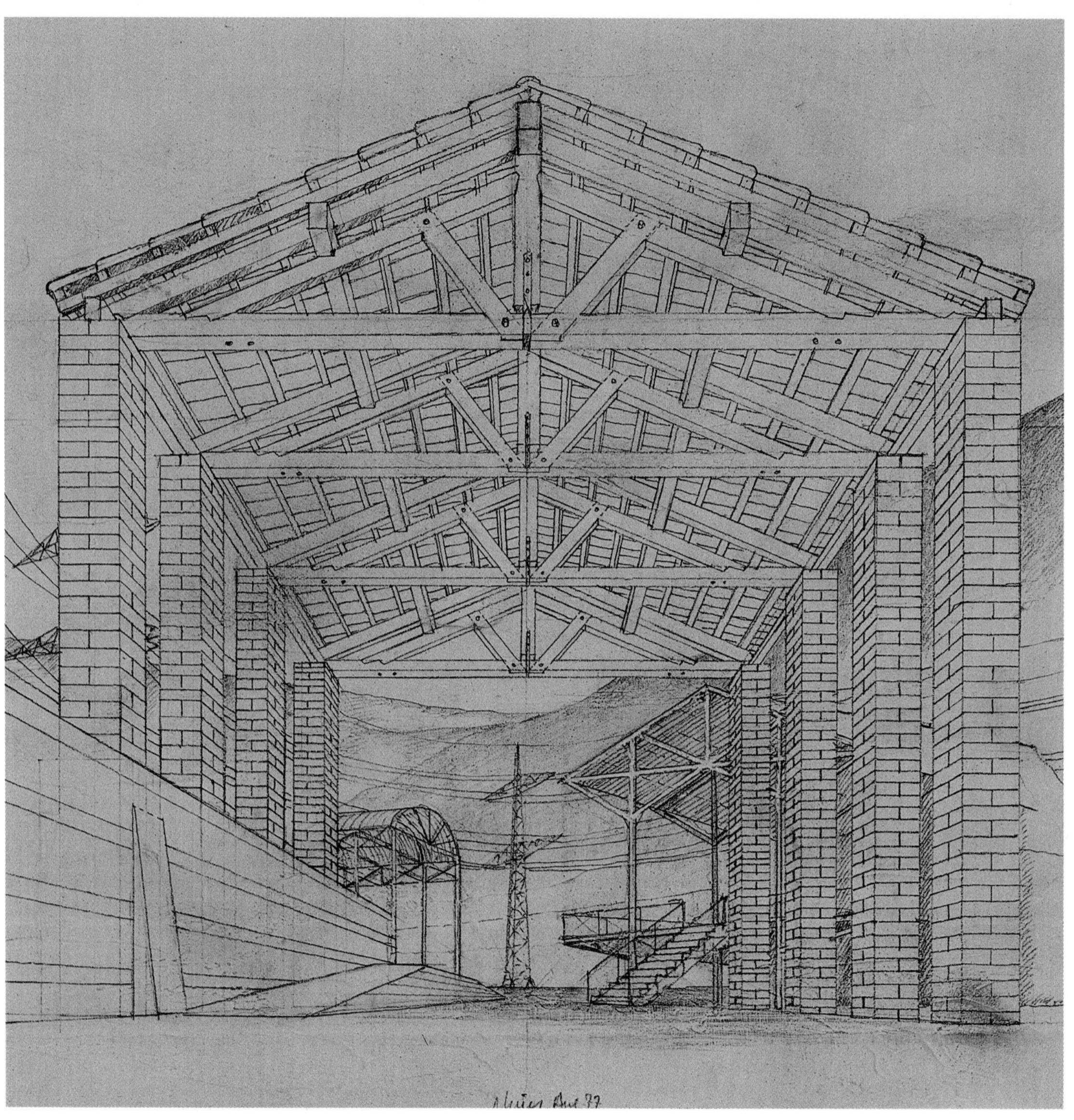

architectural theme which has lost none of its importance today, enabling dramatic inter- or counterplay between the most essential architectural elements.

The House

The enclosing and protecting wall, the differentiation of rooms inside, windows as sources of light, doors as entrances and exits, the roof to keep out the rain and cold . . . all this, thematically, technically or in the architectural aesthetic need no longer be called into question today. The

unconcern with which a deep-rooted tradition, down even to the craftsmen's skills, was destroyed in the 1920s has left wounds that will never heal. We must start again, learning to build from the fundamentals.

The Interior

The spaces inside the building, nests we paper and decorate for our daily comfort, the small objects which fill our lives with warmth and nostalgia—this is our second skin and we allow no-one, not even the best of artists, to force it on us. The architect creates the shell, the geometrical

background, which is dead until its inhabitants fill it with life. But this does not relieve him of the obligation to give his houses as full and intensive a form as possible, so that they become a well-modulated sounding-board for everyday life.

The City

The geometry of the single house derives its force from the contrast with living nature. The greater the density and number of houses, the greater the displacement of nature and the environment and thus the more important the artificial spaces, which run through the city like

canals, become. Streets and squares are the vehicles of public life, while quiet cells in the form of courtyards are places of refuge, intimacy and retreat. The architecture of residential and office buildings should be normal and decent. Only monumental buildings need particular magnificence.

Architecture and Sculpture

Since ancient times, the abstract geometrical background of buildings and urban architecture has been enriched by the contrast with figural and pictorial representations and sculpture. Since the

visual arts rejected this form of expression and began to compete with the abstraction of buildings this contrapuntal dimension has been lost.

Stele for Schinkelplatz in Berlin

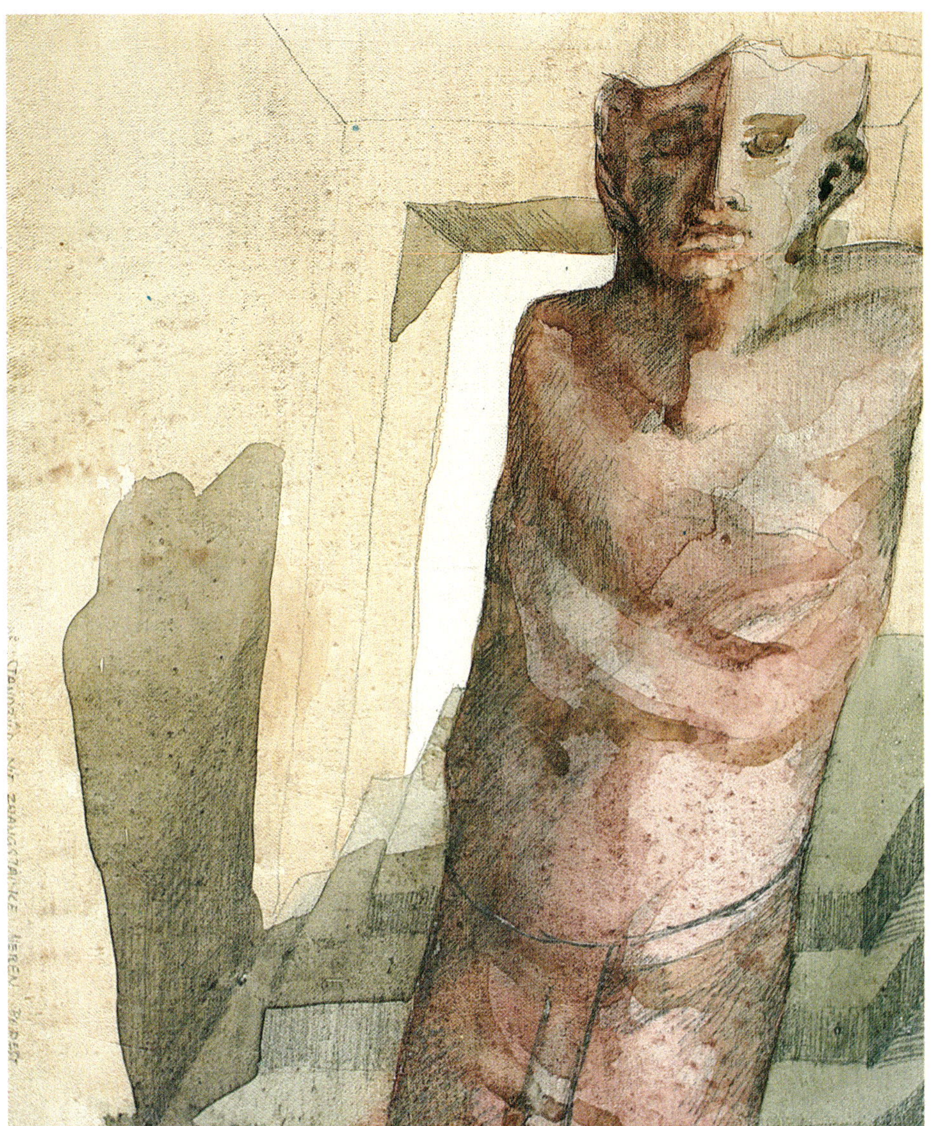

These figures are the dreams with which I adorn my evenings.

Kolbeinsson House, Luxembourg 1975

In type, this house is reminiscent of the traditional basilica with a nave and side-aisles leading into each other. The hierarchic ground-plan affords great flexibility

without detriment to the central living area. The upper rooms may also have an internal visual relation to the living room. The glass roof creates an atmosphere similar to that of a stretch of the street or an inner court.

Weidemann House, Stuttgart 1975

This house was to be built with a graphics workshop on a very steep terraced northern slope. The design was rejected by the contractor because of its 'monumentality'. In type, it is similar to the Kolbeinsson House. The storey with

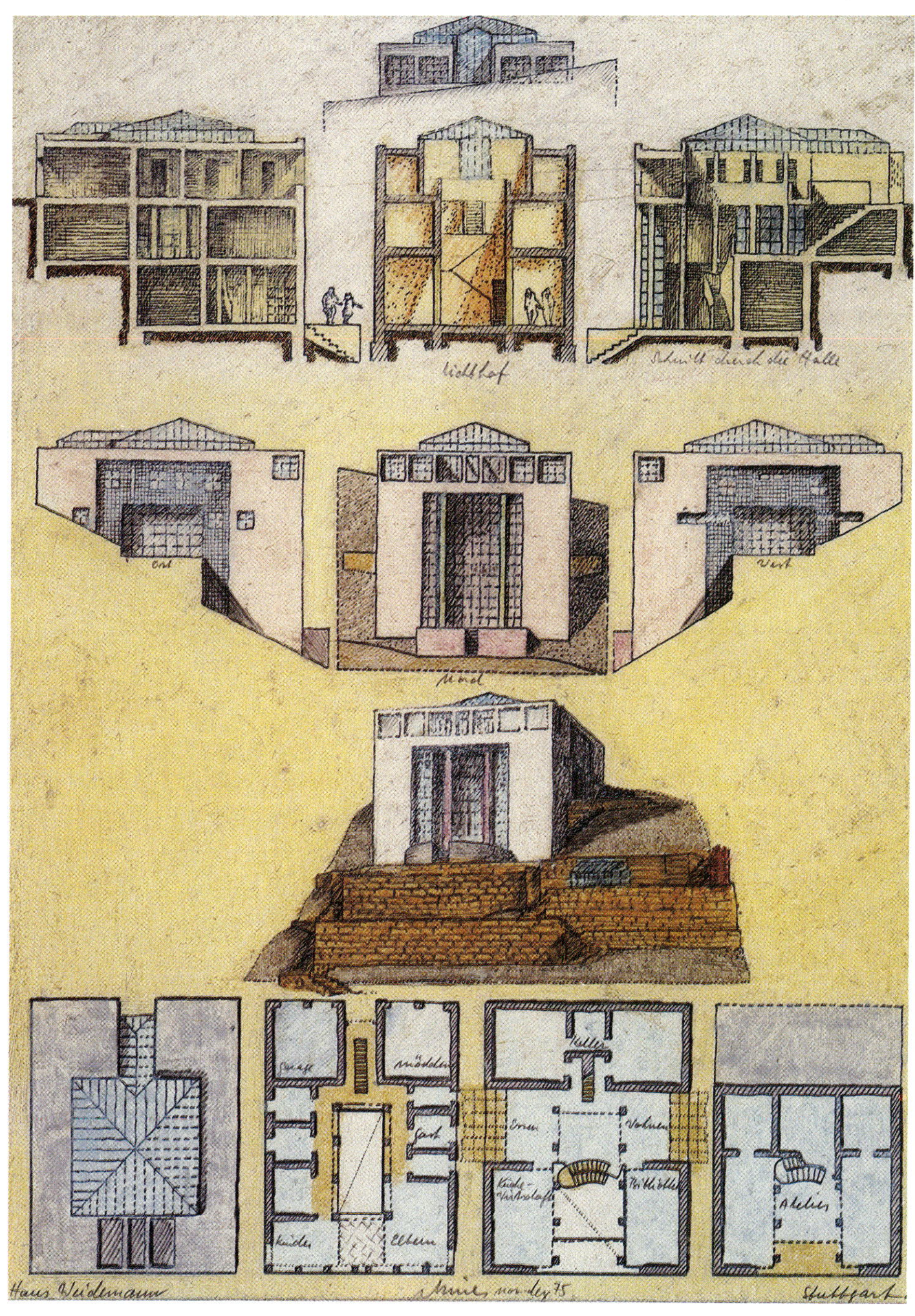

the living accommodation has a clear east-west orientation which continues on the terraces. The steps of the slope are also manifest in the three-storey space (inner court) above the studio. They are linked with various kinds of stairs.

New Community Centre, Brunn am Gebirge near Vienna 1977

This complex is to close the courtyard behind the town-hall and create a spatially intact figure. The square main hall with surrounding corridors, the stage area, the oval

stairwell and the old hall form a sequence of spaces which develops from the foyer on the ground floor. The individual parts are geometrically differentiated and linked together with joint-like articulations.

The main room and surrounding area. The individual side-walls emphasise the orientation and filter the light sources.

Cross-section through the main hall and ground floor foyer.

The oval glass-roofed staircase. The octagonal support with its mushroom capital carries the landing on the upper storey.

The link between the staircase and the old hall. The old hall has been enriched with a gallery.

High School, Perchtoldsdorf near Vienna 1977

The arrangement round a courtyard is an adaptation of the type of court or street house familiar in Lower Austria and the Burgenland. The diagonal site between the existing school buildings (*left*) and a chapel with a Biedermeier villa (*right*) is orientated towards the old village centre (a

contribution from my assistant, Mr. Gaugusch). The courtyard used during breaks has a glass roof and cuts through the body of the building at a slight angle. This is continued outside in an existing avenue of trees and a bridge construction which links the new building with the old.

The entrance facade is embedded between the existing buildings and protected by beautiful old trees.

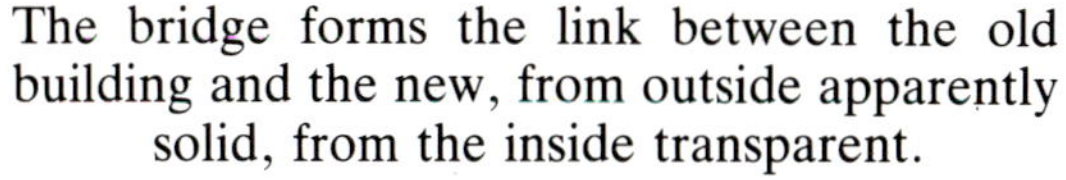

The bridge forms the link between the old building and the new, from outside apparently solid, from the inside transparent.

The courtyard with the view onto the gymnasium. The facades differ according to their function.

The courtyard with the view onto the music pavilion. The courtyard with its glass roof is in the background behind the solid wall.

The Glass-Roofed Courtyard

This lies between the administrative area, the library and the classrooms and serves as a playground protected from the weather, a general hall, exhibition space and meeting-place. The

glass roof is convex. The supporting structure is conceived in three sections; the centre section has a multi-storey flight of stairs at one side.

The Facade Composition

All sections of the facade are designed to reflect the function of the rooms behind them, so that any layman will be able to tell from outside where the main or side entrance is, and where the

classrooms, corridors and toilets are located. The classrooms on the ground floor will be more shaded by the trees than those on the upper floors and so have larger windows.

Residential Area 'Rennweg', Vienna 1977

On the fringe of the southern section of the city the Baroque 'Rennweg' barracks still stand between two main arterial roads. It was proposed to create a complex of 800 apartments here. In my design, I preserved all the valuable parts of the old buildings, adapting them for modern use,

while the 'superblock' was intersected with normal streets so as to blend into the surrounding area. A broad grassed area forms the centrepiece of the new complex.

The street and gateway. The blocks should be divided in such a way that several different architects can be commissioned to work on small units of houses.

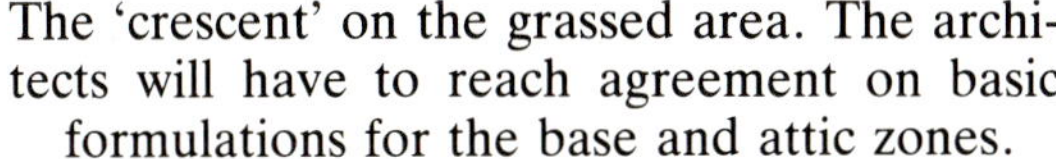

The 'crescent' on the grassed area. The architects will have to reach agreement on basic formulations for the base and attic zones.

All the designers should work to the same gutter height. Economic considerations will contribute much to an harmonisation of the houses.

The great variety of architecture in the city has always been to its enrichment.

Sketches for Variations on the Facade Composition

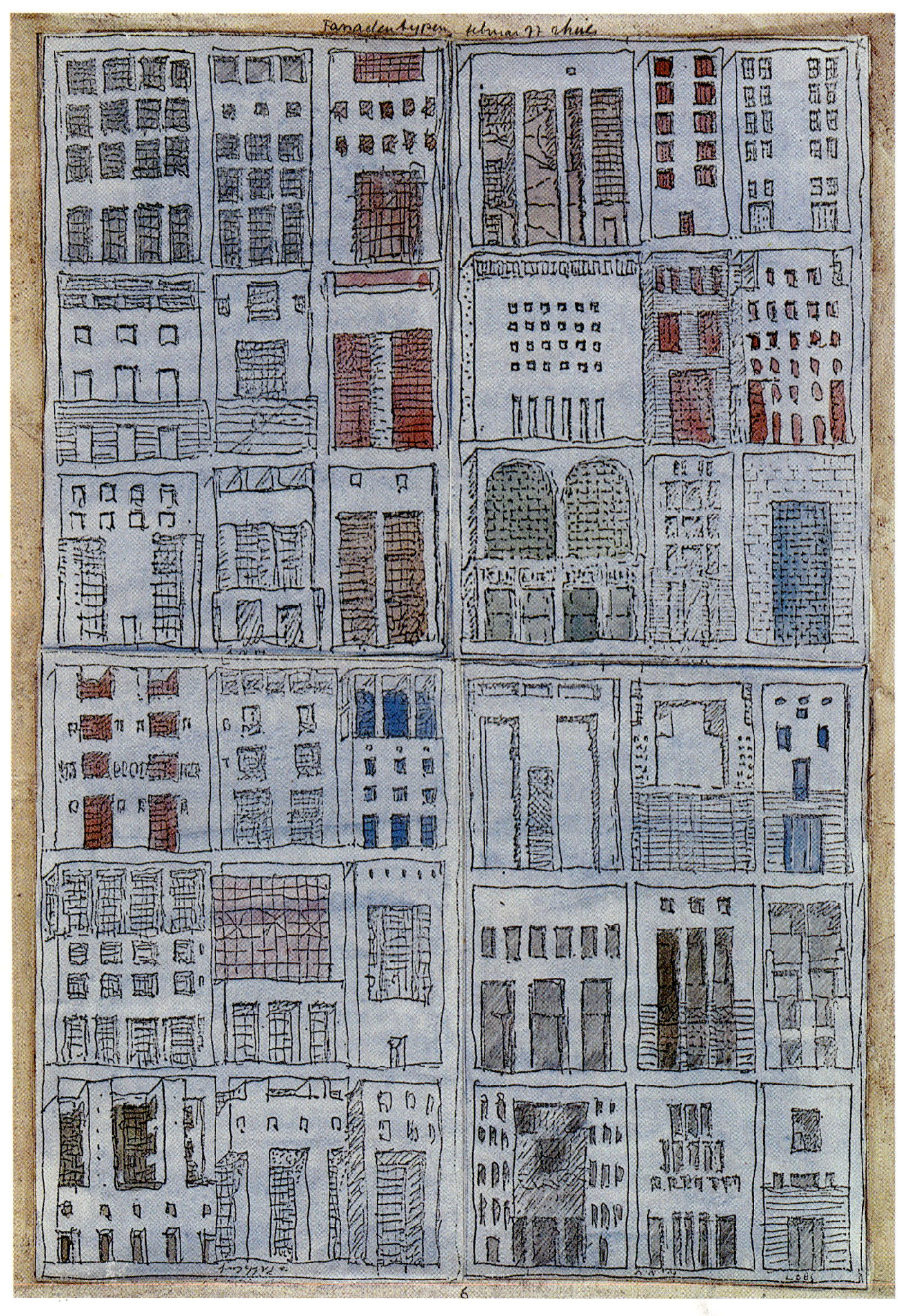

Sketches on the Theme of the Corner House

Site Plan for a Village in the Burgenland, Austria 1977

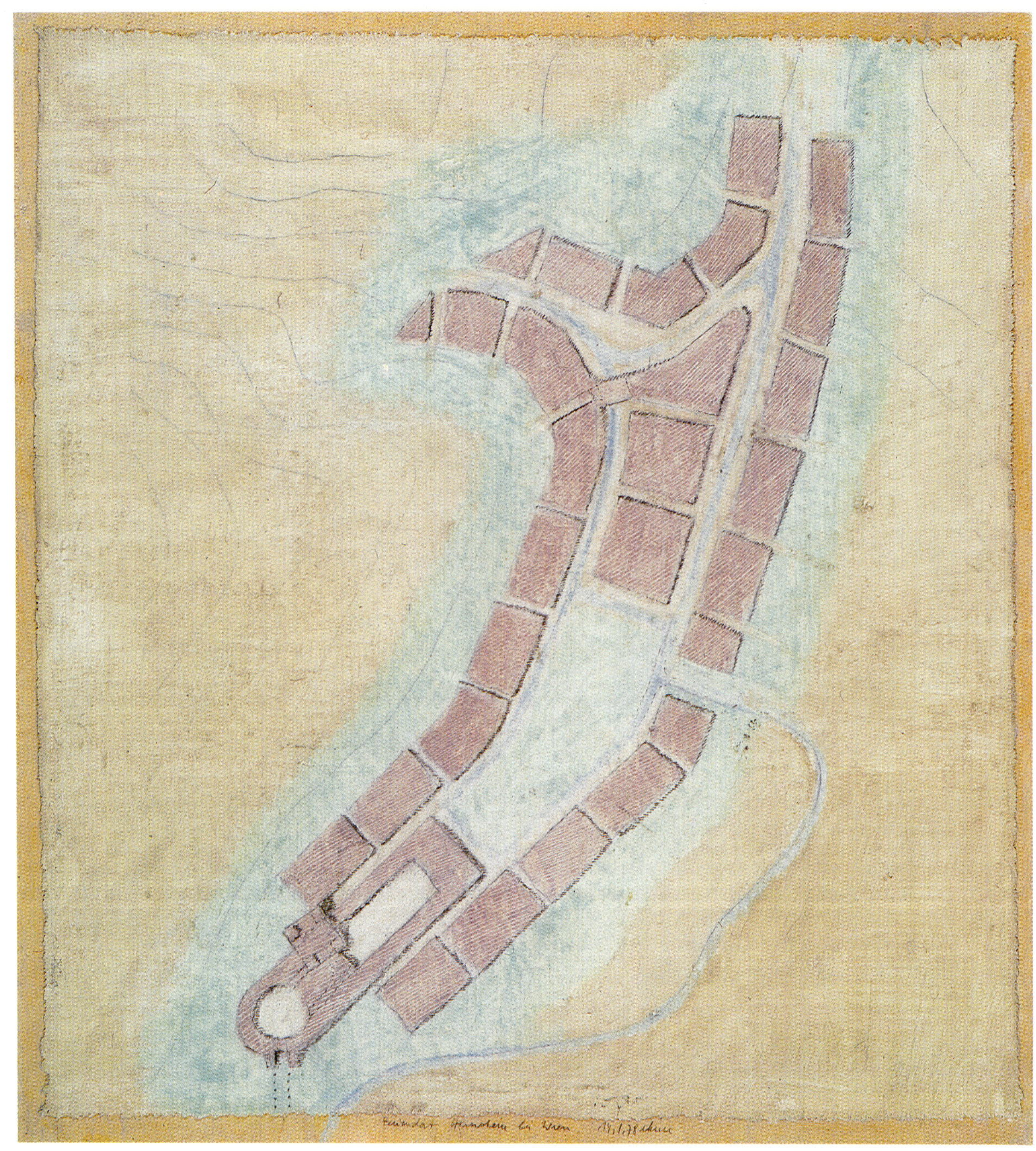

The village nestles on the crest of a ridge. In structure it follows the traditional pattern of the district, being grouped around a large central green planted with trees.

Details of the Village Structure

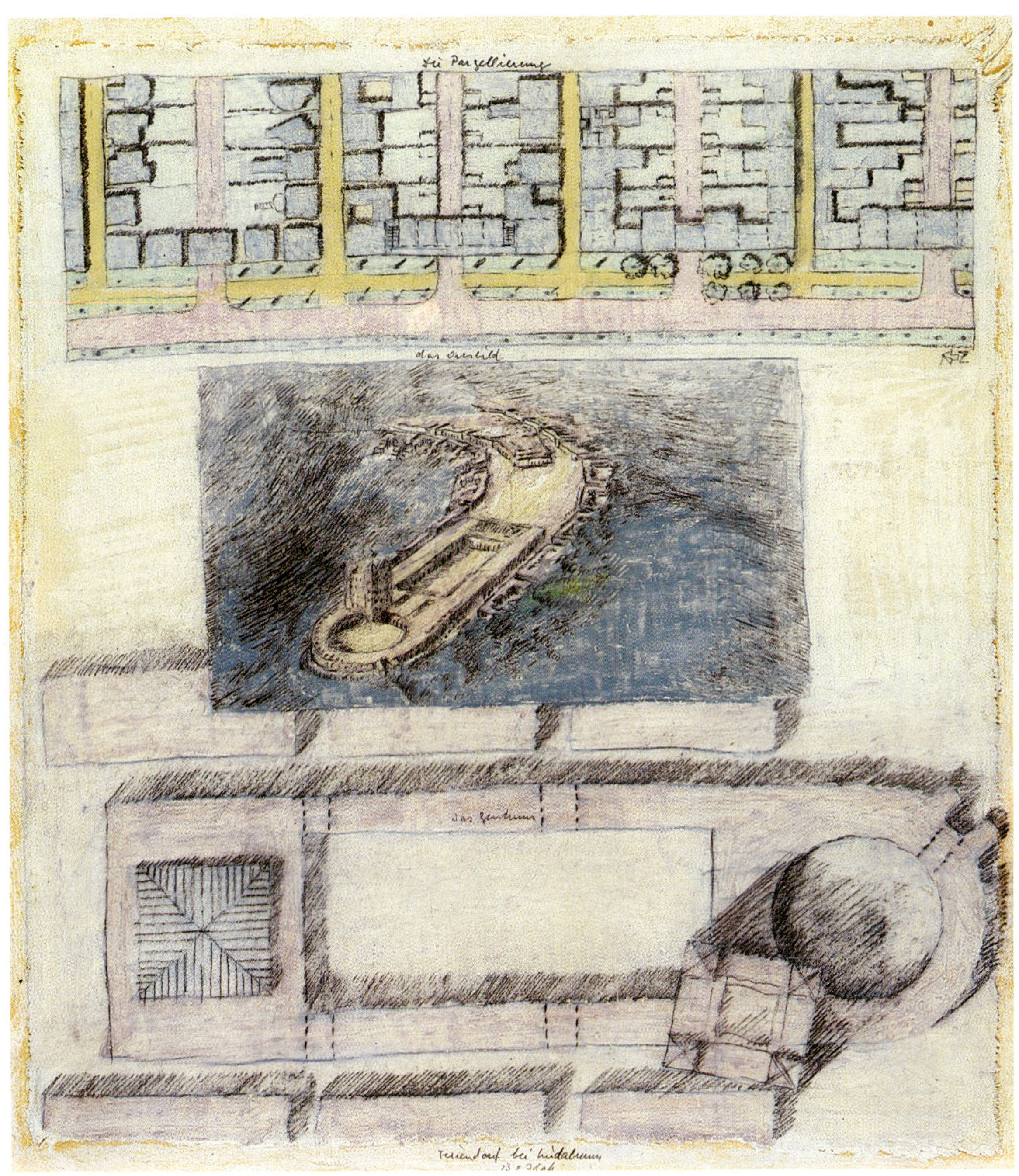

The houses form a comb-like shape around the green. Those built in an L- or U-shape are an adaptation of the traditional local house-type. The public buildings are grouped in a complex at the head of the village.

Hamburg Altona-Nord 1978

The district around the former Opera House is to be renovated during the next few years. The main

elements of this plan can be incorporated into the building scheme which has now been accepted by the municipal authorities.

The existing lay-out (*top left*); the new block division with streets from my design (*top right*); the main accents of the new composition (*bottom*).

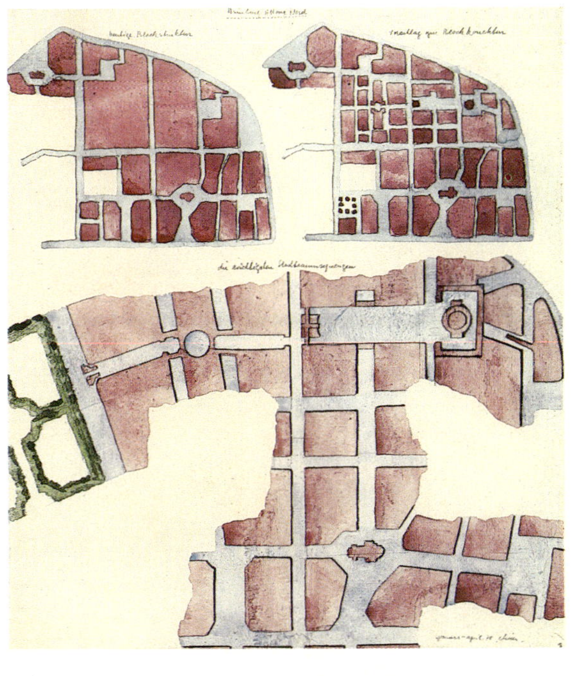

The existing circular structure of the Schiller-Oper is given a new mantle and becomes a multi-purpose building. The space is paved to contrast with the grassed area and surrounded by an arcade.

A round space in front of the old people's home—a place to meet.

The grassed area with indoor sports hall and Bolzplatz.

Residential and Office Block on the former Pferdemarkt, Hamburg Altona-Nord

This building was changed completely during the course of the project. The round space in front

of the old people's home was jettisoned and this is my attempt at re-interpretation. This building serves as a gateway to the overall composition.

Residential and Office Block on the former Pferdemarkt

A two-storey residential area is to be built on the roof of the block, orientated entirely to the

interior to minimise the traffic noise. The lower drawing shows the rear facade of the apartments, which all look down onto the central circular area. The apartments are two-storey.

The Shopping Arcade between the Pferdemarkt and the Opera House

The axis cuts close to the Opera House and affords a view into the ensuing area. The corners are

marked with towers; the passage has an arcade and terracing above to let more sunlight through to the upper apartments.

The New Borders for the Grassed Area

On the side leading to the Opera House, the grassed area is edged with projecting buildings; in

the background four towers (housing doctors' surgeries) mark the entrance to the ensuing residential area, which is very scattered and offers little scope for architectural improvement. To the left is the street opening which reveals the church and this is echoed by a conch-like opening in the row of houses on the right.

Development Phases of Südliche Friedrichstadt, Berlin

State in 1790 State in 1850

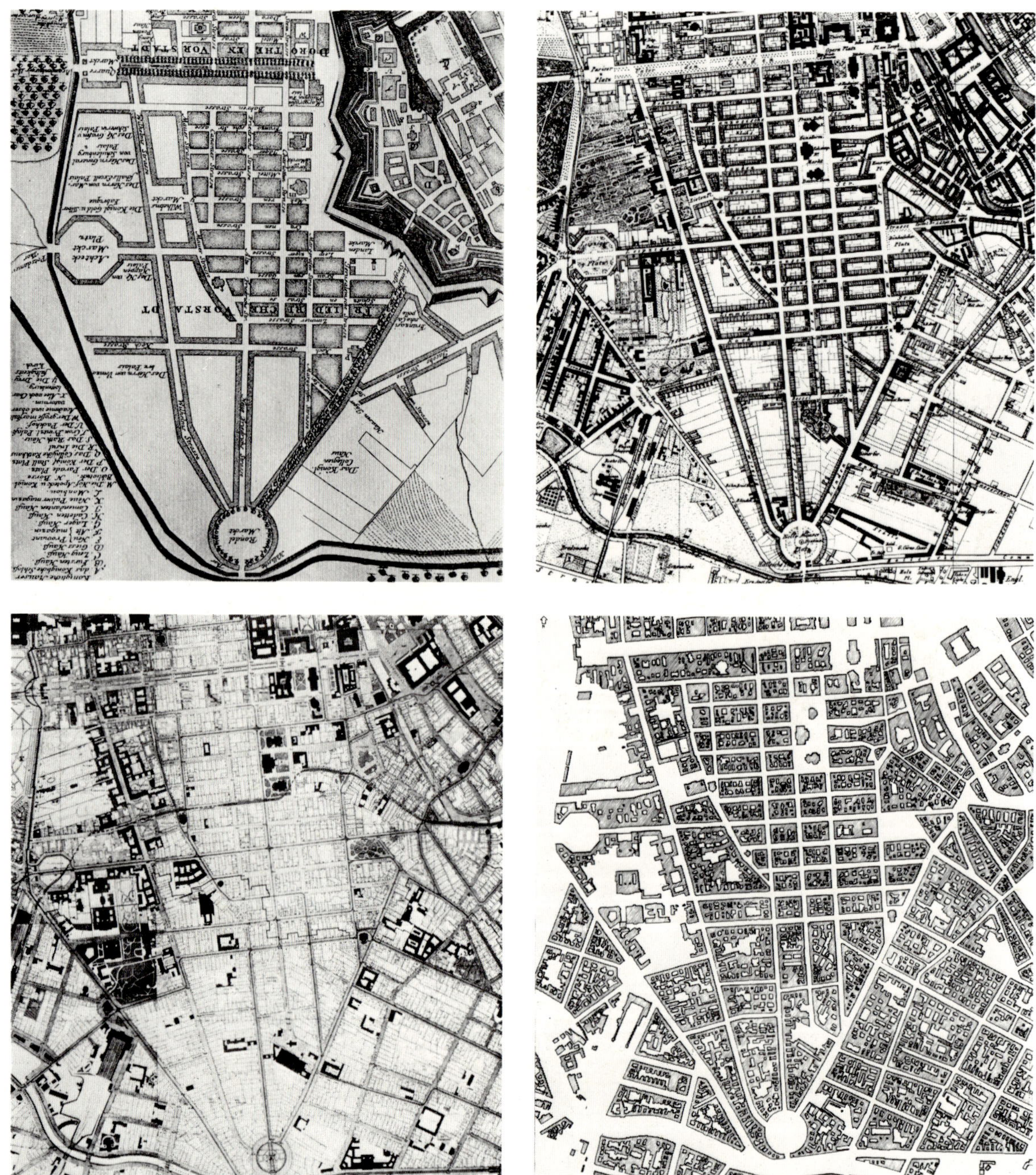

State in 1900 State in 1938

My Ideal Plan for Südliche Friedrichstadt 1977

In contrast to the development which took place here in the post-war years, I would suggest that the main accents of the old urban ground plan be respected. Corrections should be made to the gigantic blocks in the southern part (in West Berlin) in such a way that when the Wall, which cuts through the

middle of this part of the city, is pulled down there will be a typological relation between the blocks in the two sectors. The site of the Schinkelplatz and Ritterstrasse projects which are illustrated on the following pages is visible on the lower right half of this plan.

Südliche Friedrichstadt

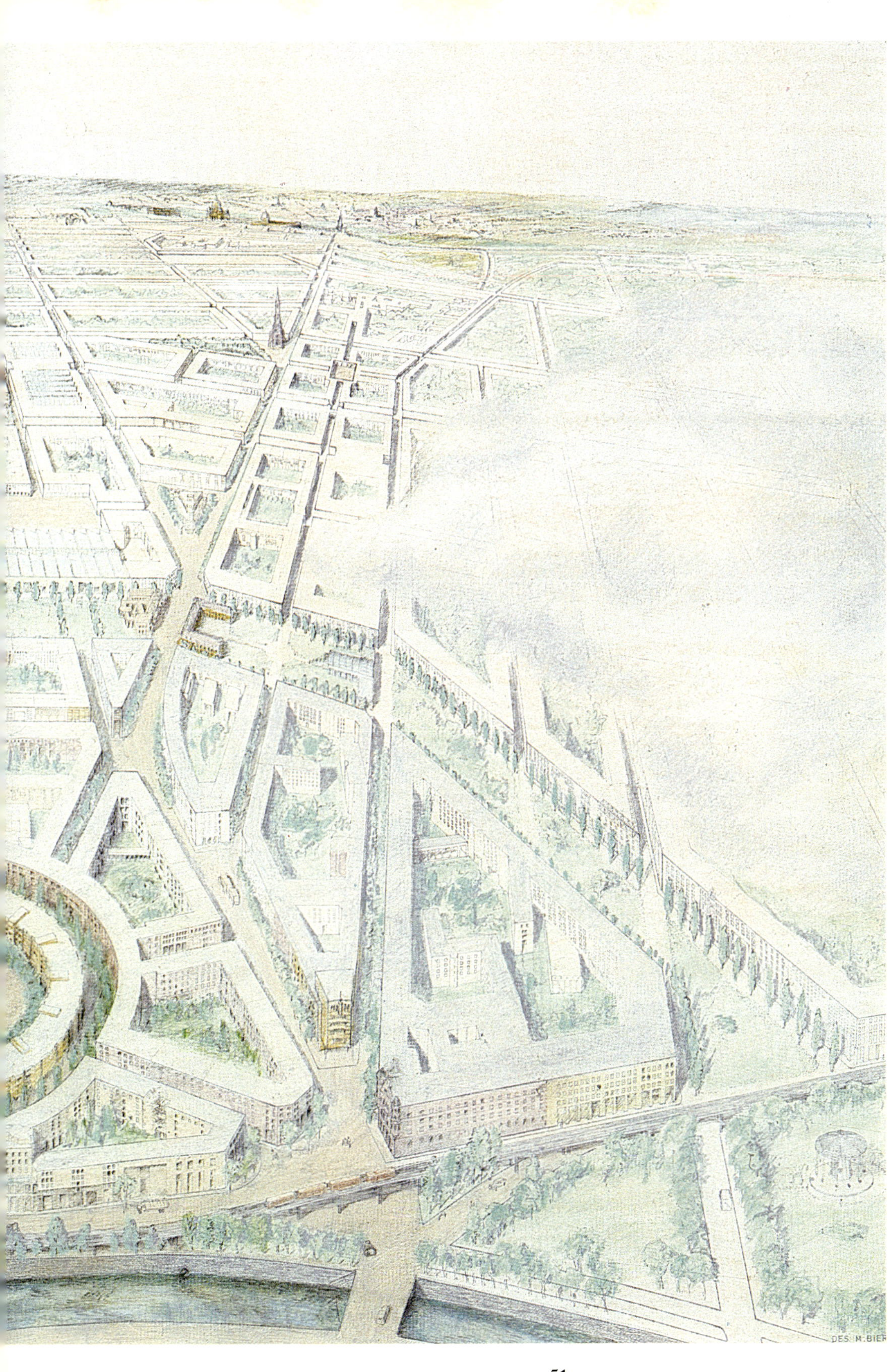

Ideal Plan 1977

Proposal 1977 for the Area Lindenstrasse, Alte Jakobstrasse and Ritterstrasse in Berlin, with Schinkelplatz at the top

The sketch shows the proportions of the blocks in Nördliche Friedrichstadt. The residential areas are approximately 40 × 50 metres, an ideal size for four-storey

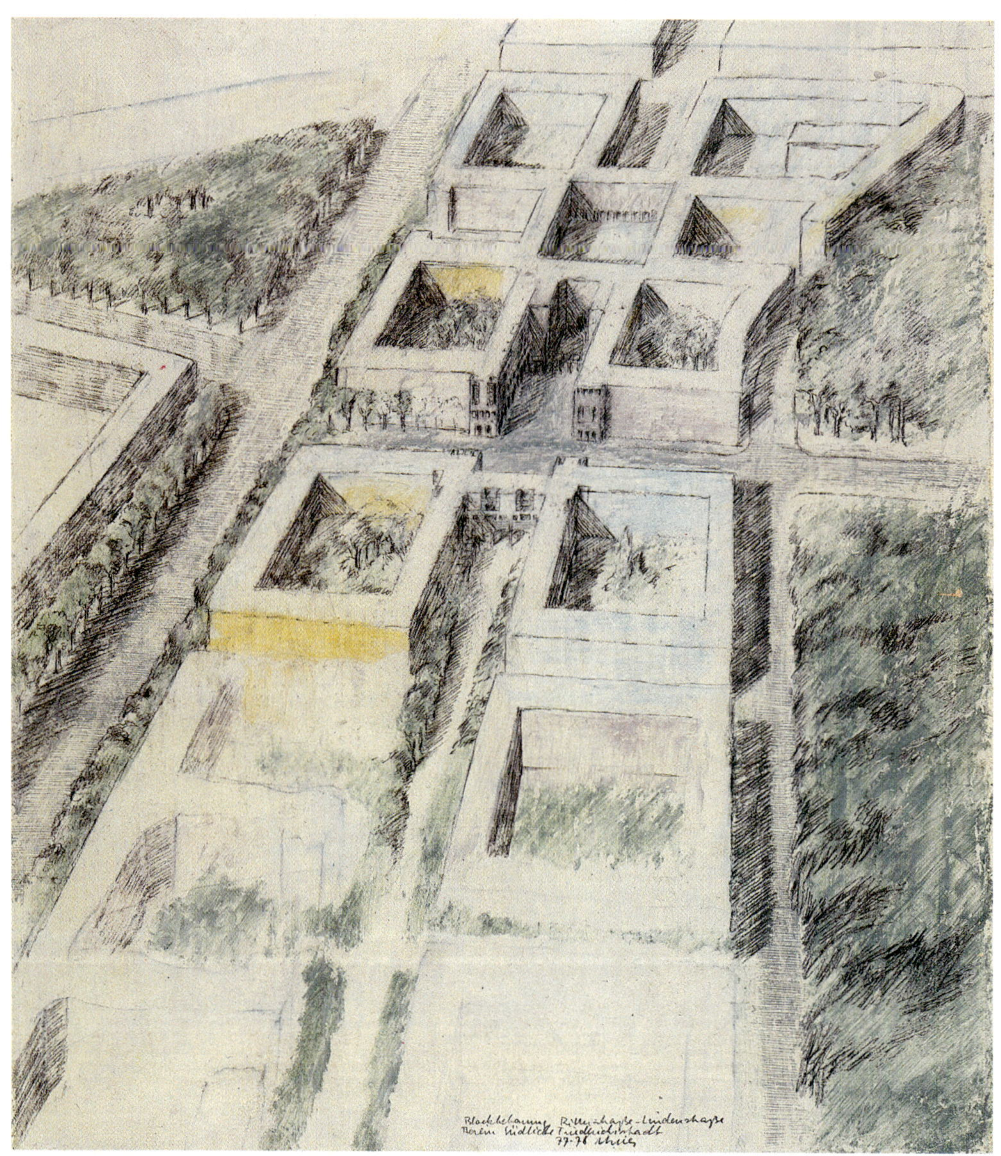

structures. The southern side of Ritterstrasse with the gate I designed is already standing. Work began on Schinkelplatz and the adjoining blocks in the summer of 1981.

In both sections I was able to achieve my aim of involving several architects.

Schinkelplatz as the Focus of Four Blocks

This is the view from the north. Where the 'traditional' facade is now visible stood the house

belonging to the ceramics manufacturer, Feilner, who commissioned the design from Schinkel. Sadly the house was destroyed in the last war. I regard it as legitimate to recall its noble facade with simple means today.

Schinkelplatz, Berlin 1977–81

The square is closed on all sides to give maximum spatial intimacy. It is to form the main accent in a composition which develops from Oranienstrasse to the Berlin Museum. The ground plans vary from one apartment to the next in such a way that the

basic type remains the same and only the geometry of the living space changes. As this is a project for the International Building Exhibition in Berlin, it is legitimate in my view to experiment and test the varying qualities of the different geometries in close sequence.

The Facades on Schinkelplatz

Three facades of the square are identical. They consist of a two-storey base in the form of an arcade with an attic storey set back. This is to make the square, which is small (30 × 30 metres) seem larger. The 'Feilner facade' is not a copy of Schinkel's

design, it merely respects the proportions of the windows, the gateway, and the attic. The facades on the streets which lead into the square are all different to facilitate orientation.

Designs for Facade Compositions on Schinkelplatz

Designs for Facade Compositions on Schinkelplatz

Right: Facades on Feilnerstrasse and the north-south passage.

Designs for Facades on Schinkelplatz

Designs for Facades on Schinkelplatz

These sketches were stuck onto cardboard and set up in the form of a square to enable a better assessment of their effect.

Sketches for the Corners of Schinkelplatz

Sketches for the Corners of Schinkelplatz

The classical handling of corners to courtyards or squares requires the material to become more dense towards the corner. Here, however, it needs to be broken up as there are terraces and living spaces behind.

Sketches for the Residential Accommodation on Schinkelplatz

Sketches for the Residential Accommodation on Schinkelplatz

The classical spatial geometries are neutral and can be used independently of time and culture. These typologies could be very much extended. In the combination of different sizes of room and geometries lies 'true art...'

Building with 23 Apartments in Ritterstrasse, Südliche Friedrichstadt, Berlin 1977–80

Ground floor plan

First floor plan

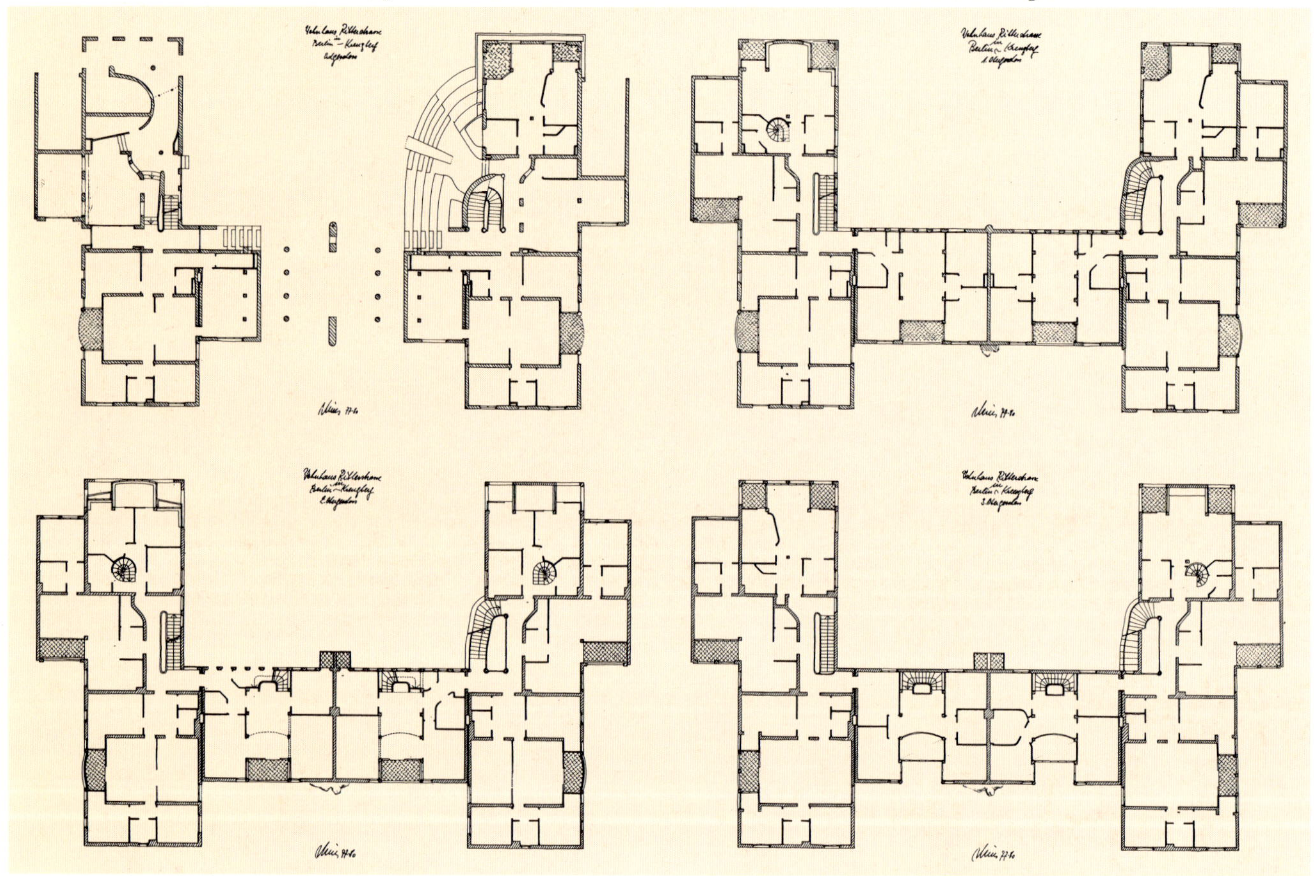

Second floor plan

Third floor plan

Sketches for the Facades of the Projecting Buildings on Ritterstrasse

The Building seen from Ritterstrasse

As the street facade faces north, the apartments in the projecting buildings had to open as far as possible to the east and west. The stairs and utility rooms are in the shaded zones. On the street,

the projections give emphasis to the court-like niche while the low arch spans the street. This is to be continued later in the interior of the block as a small alley.

The Building seen from the Courtyard

The windows on the frontage can be walled up later when the alley is built. The sculpture over the arch is a winged figure, naturalistic in the lower part but becoming more abstract towards the head. The body and wings merge into the stonework.

Building on Ritterstrasse, Berlin
Apartment on a Turkish Ground Plan

Since so many Turks live in Kreuzberg I wanted to use a traditional Turkish ground plan with a glazed veranda. Regrettably the rent was too high for any of

the Turks to be able to take it. This is a two-storey apartment which like a cell can stand alone or be included in a complex.

Building on Ritterstrasse, Berlin
6-Room Apartment

This ground plan derives from the type used for the Kolbeinsson House. The

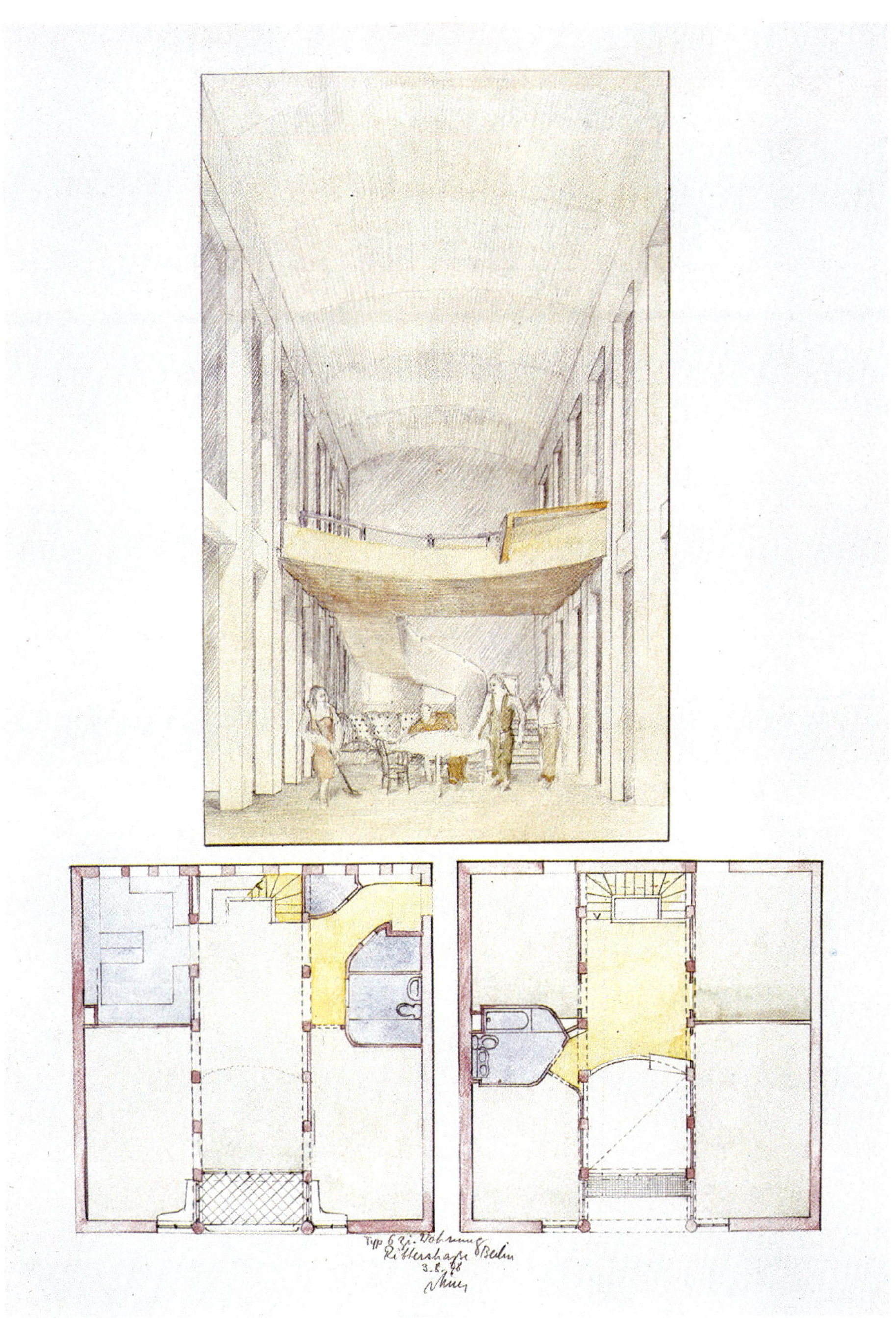

skeletal interior permits maximum variability. All the living rooms on the top floor have barrel vaulted ceilings to indicate the proximity of the roof.

Ephraim Palais, Lindenstrasse, Berlin 1979

The right wing of the palace stood in what is now the eastern part of the city, but was demolished before the war. After the war the numbered stones were re-discovered in West Berlin, and the Senate has now decided to rebuild the palace for the Jewish community and provide cultural

facilities there. The work presents a special challenge in the handling of valuable historical material and the best approach would appear to be a plain solid structure with the same proportions as the old building. The junction of the old and new sections should be bridged with a glazed foyer and stairs.

Rear Facade of the Ephraim Palais

From the central part of the foyer zone a semi-circular lecture room projects into the courtyard area. Ramps are attached which link the lecture hall with the garden. The main compositional

element of the old palace was the oval salon with an oval staircase. I have attempted to create a 'twin' to the Baroque predecessor through a similar sequence on the new corner.

Open-Air Theatre, Breitscheidplatz, Berlin 1978

This design emerged from a number of different proposals. The arcades which lead inwards and the ramp outside are to protect the theatre, which is sunk below ground level, from noise.

Open-Air Theatre, Breitscheidplatz

A glass gallery conceals the commercial facade of the Europa Centre with all its advertisements. A mobile tent roof, of the kind used by Frei Otto, can be rolled out from the glass roof to protect the

audience in bad weather. The glass wall can also be covered with a projection screen. The theatre could therefore be used for the film festival.

Prager Platz, Berlin 1978

The square still bears the marks of the war. I would suggest restoring the original ground plan as far as possible. The projections where the streets meet the square are to increase the architectural

frontage. Moreover, the best apartments can be placed at these corners. In the interior of the block (upper left on the plan) a large swimming pool is to be built, together with an adult education centre, a day nursery, library, restaurant, etc.

Prager Platz

Here too the buildings are not to be designed by one architect but as in all my urban projects be worked out in collaboration with several colleagues. I have tried here to simulate the result.

Sketches showing the Architectural Development of Prager Platz

Sketches for the Interiors of Prager Platz

Top left to bottom right: the inner court in the adult education centre; the glass-covered circular area, focus of all the activities; the square court in the day nursery; the glass galleries which lead to the

interior; the geometry of the square; the frigidarium; the big swimming pool; the caldarium and a paddling pool for children. Each area has its individual geometry.

House Types for Prager Platz

House Types for Prager Platz

House at Lindenufer 34, Berlin Spandau 1978

The design of this house is spartan and simple. The utility rooms are in a central tower section which has a plain pierced facade. The windows are

proportioned on a golden section, becoming slightly smaller from one storey to the next.

House on Lindenufer

The entrance is a trapezium and leads through a small intermediary area to the oval stairwell. A hexagonal pavilion leads from here into the garden. The living room and dining room are set sideways to the body of the

building and so enjoy better lighting. The hall is made to seem shorter through the trumpet-shaped opening to the living room. All the bedrooms face south.

House at Lindenufer N-31, Berlin Spandau 1979

Preliminary studies for the entire row.

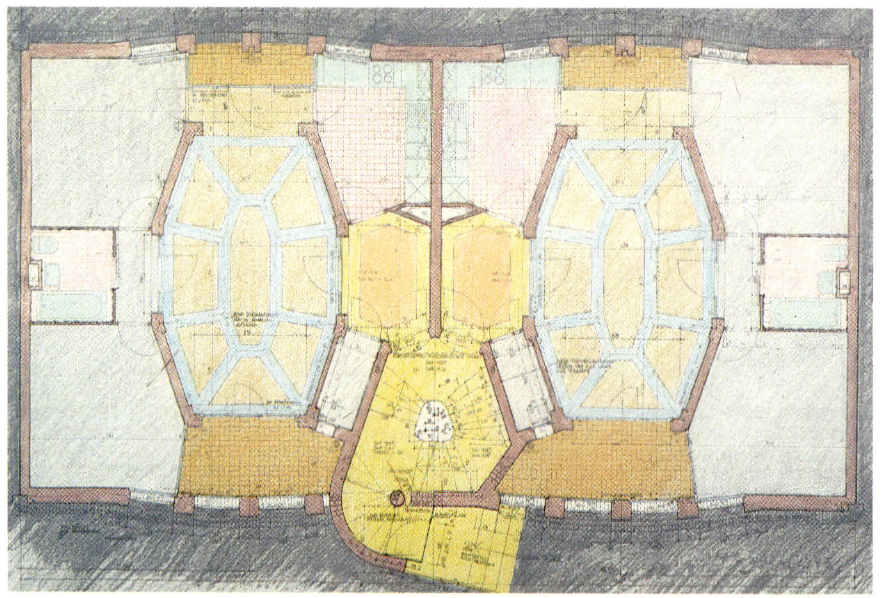

Ground-plan with octagonal living room, hexagonal hall and septagonal stairwell. This geometrical progression develops naturally out of the design of the living room.

Alternative with pergola.

The Octagonal Living Room

Geometrically the room opens inwards, giving greater space where it is most needed. The room has a winter garden facing south which acts as a compensatory climatic zone.

Re-Design of the 'Via Triumphalis', Karlsruhe 1979

Present state | New design

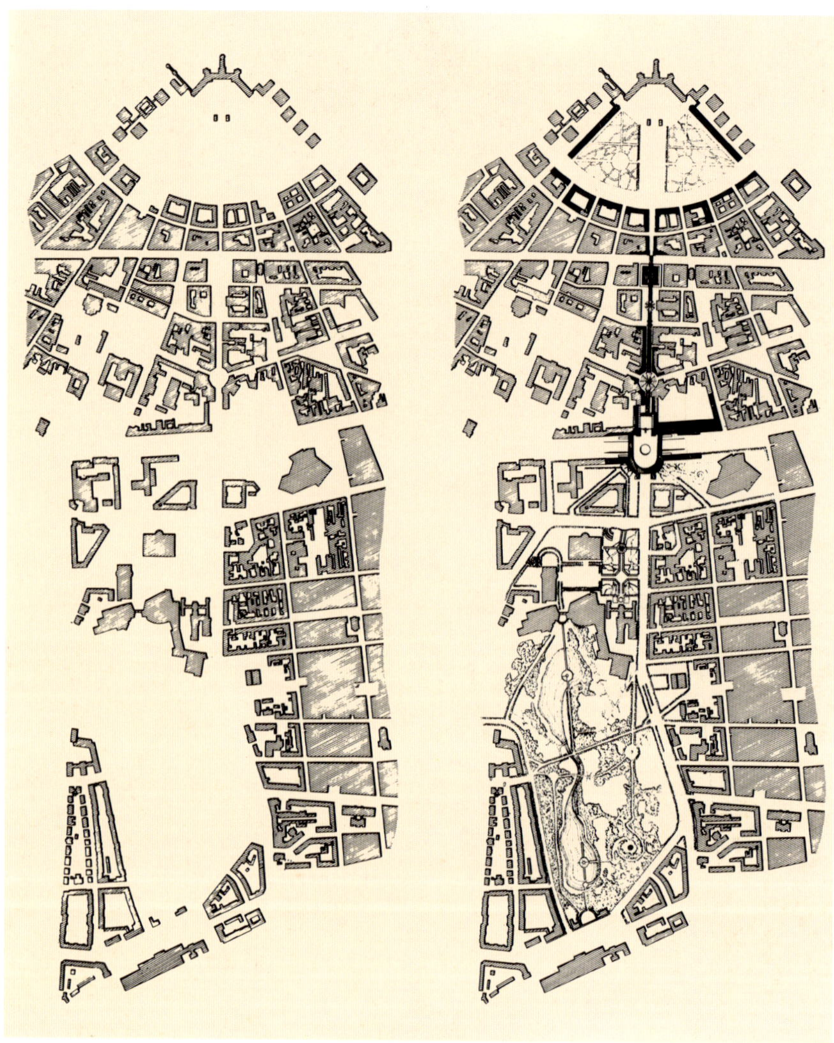

My proposals concentrate on (*from top to bottom*): the square in front of the palace, the market place, the circus, Ettlinger Torplatz, Festplatz, the public paths through the zoo and the re-designed area in front of the railway station.

Market Place, Karlsruhe

The Neoclassical architect, Weinbrenner, who built the market place at the beginning of the 19th century, wanted

to have two U-shaped market halls in the front part of the square. The city council has taken this idea up again and asked me to present a design.

The Market Place in Karlsruhe looking towards the Palace

The rear facades on Kaiserstrasse (in yellow) are corrections to facades dating from the 1950s. The ghastly advertisements which disfigure these houses from top to bottom should be confined to the ground floor.

The Circus in Karlsruhe

On the left in the background is Weinbrenner's Kurfürsten palace. Here too I would suggest improving the bad facades of the post-war years without impairing the function of the houses or affecting their construction.

The Composition of the Open Market Halls

The arched outside wall reflects the base of Weinbrenner's building. It is in the same sandstone.

Towards thę centre of the square the transparency of both the elements and the material changes.

The New Ettlinger Torplatz

In place of the old Neoclassical gateway by Weinbrenner with its radiating division of the routes into the southern parts of the city we now have a section of the city Autobahn. I would suggest building

the little square above this irreparable anti-city nightmare to create a relatively pleasant space for pedestrians and to link the old city boundary with the adjoining districts.

Greenery for an Underground Garage beneath Festplatz in Karlsruhe

Wrought-iron work making green arbours

A green dome as focal point

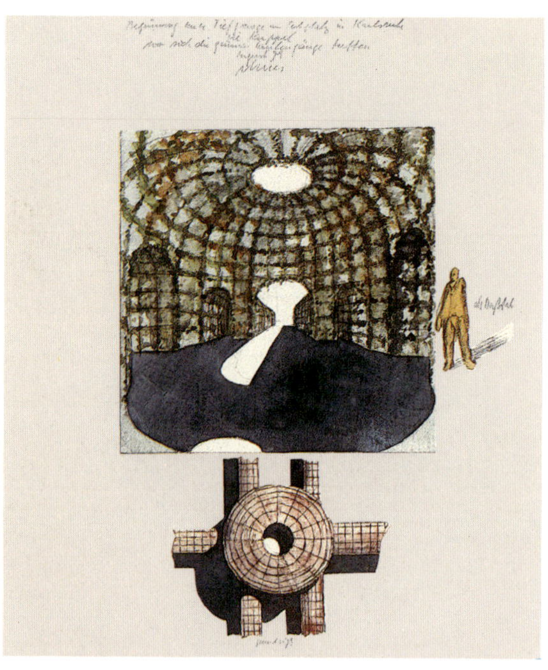

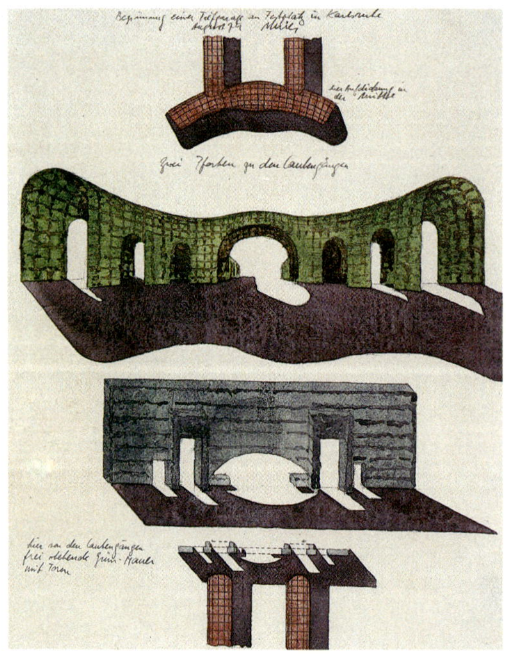

Portals leading into the arbours

Tea Pavilion on the Lake in the middle of the Zoo

The moorings for the boats follow the axis of the line of trees which leads in a straight line from the station to the Festplatz.

Library, Karlsruhe 1979

The site is opposite Weinbrenner's Church of St Stephan. This has had a major influence on the design. Fragments of old buildings have been so incorporated that the transitions are scarcely evident. One example is the detached

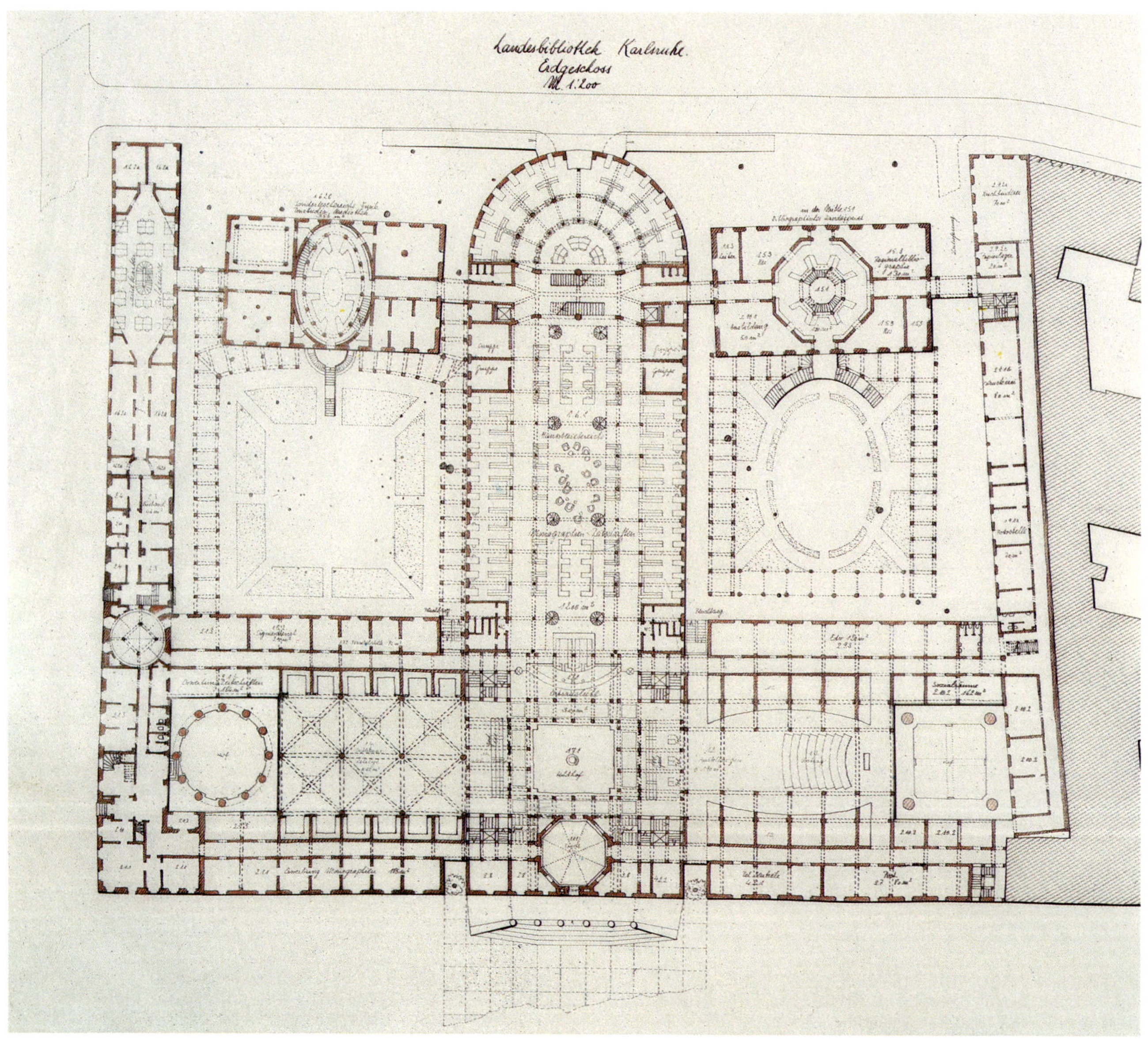

villa on the upper right, which stands at a slight angle to the street. I have responded to this by constructing the same building at a similar angle on the left and incorporating it into the complex as a whole.

Library, Karlsruhe

The large reading rooms are conceived as three different types of construction. The main room has a vaulted ceiling without supports, the left-hand room has two aisles, the right three. All the rooms have small study areas

along their sides. The green courts can also be used as reading space in the summer. The visual appearance has been varied as much as possible throughout to facilitate orientation.

Sketches for the Interior of the Library

Top left to bottom right: ground plan, main entrance, foyer, glass-covered court and local lending library, staircase and main reading room.

Sketches for the Interior of the Library

Variants of the main reading room with its conch-like end, the two-aisled reading room with its galleries, the three-aisled reading room and the courts which let in the light.

Mon enfant, ma soeur,
Songe à la douceur
D'aller là-bas vivre ensemble! . . .

Là, tout n'est qu'ordre et beauté,
Luxe, calme et volupté.

From Baudelaire's 'L'Invitation au Voyage', *Les Fleurs du Mal*